WINDCHAT

RIDGE

LIFE SECRETS OF A

TRAVELLING SONGBIRD

STEVE J SMITH

Published by Saron Publishers in 2025

ISBN-13: 978-1-913297-63-3
Also available as an ebook
978-1-913297-64-0

Saron Publishers
Pwllmeyrick House
Mamhilad
Mon
NP4 8RG

saronpublishers.co.uk
info@saronpublishers.co.uk
Follow us on Facebook and Twitter

WHINCHAT RIDGE

LIFE SECRETS OF A TRAVELLING SONGBIRD

STEVE J SMITH

To my wife Alyson

WHINCHAT RIDGE

INDEX

Preface

Whinchat Ridge is a collection of facts and anecdotes gathered by one man with a lifetime's obsession with one of Britain's lesser-known songbirds: the whinchat. Many hours of field work over more than three and a half decades, using eccentric methods of stealth and field craft, has led to his accumulating all the information required to produce this work.

This book looks at the life biology of the whinchat, as well as some of the other species that share its habitat on the moorland edge. The landscape and the flora are just as important as the species that live there so there are chapters on both. The work has a local flavour that mentions local place names and would appeal to those readers who have only a general interest as well as to ornithologists and nature lovers.

The Author

Living in the eastern valley of Gwent all his life, Steve has had an interest in natural history, particularly birds, since early childhood. This interest gathered momentum with maturity and he began to study birds in greater depth. He has been a licenced bird ringer with the British Trust for Ornithology for many years. Steve has contributed to many journals and books by other writers and has become an authority on the whinchat in Wales. He is also a keen photographer and artist as well as a part-time shepherd, helping to preserve rare breed sheep. He is a recently retired countryside ranger and he describes his interest in the whinchat as 'obsessive' . . .

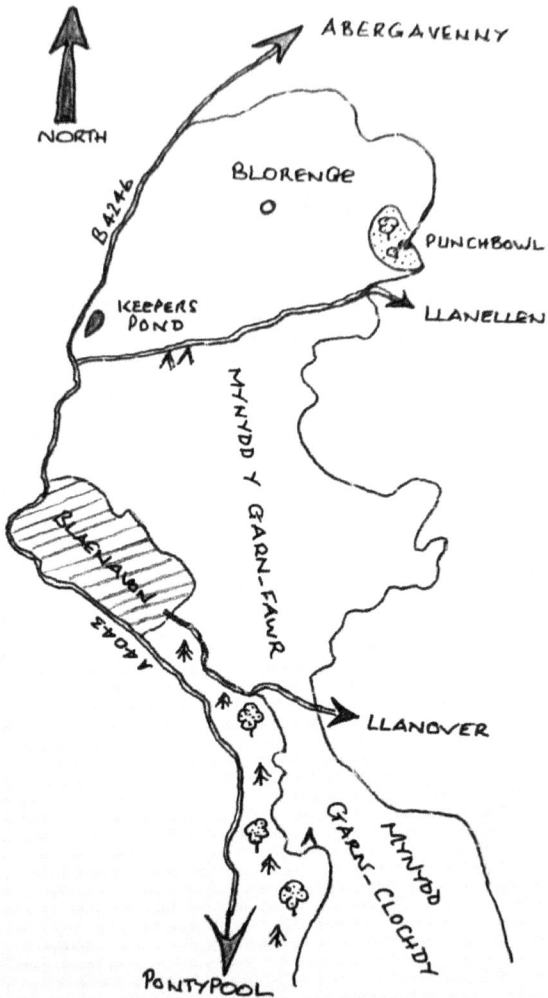

NORTH

ABERGAVENNY

B4246

BLORENGE

PUNCHBOWL

KEEPERS
POND

LLANELLEN

MYNYDD Y GARN-FAWR

BLAENAVON

A4043

LLANOVER

MYNYDD
GARN-CLOCHDY

PONTYPOOL

Introduction

The birds of the uplands and of the moorland edge have always held a special place in my heart. Born and bred in the eastern valleys of Gwent, I grew up in the shadow of the rolling hills that I was destined to fall in love with. The rich and splendid diversity of the bird life and the habitat which was their home became the icing on an already very tasty cake.

Species like the wheatear, linnet, and skylark; and the ring ouzel, red grouse and peregrine falcon have always summoned up visions of moorland landscapes with purple heather, yellow gorse, cotton grasses and others. During the winter months, the moor can be a ghostly, silent place, devoid of the hustle and bustle of the breeding songbird population of summer. However, it is always a place of inspiration as its mood changes with the seasons.

Even though many of the hillside bird species can be found in lowland habitats, somehow they seem more at home in a majestic moorland setting. Some people like to do their bird watching in woodlands; many cling to the shores and inland waters where the chances of seeing rarer birds are greater. However, for me, the hills and rocky ridges with their towering viewpoints are the places that produce inspiration within my soul.

My earliest memories of exploring the wonders of bird life are of a time when I was in junior school at Victoria Village, Abersychan. Some friends and I used to collect, in our child-like ignorance, the eggs of common species that nested in our neighbourhood and, even though my collection only reached a grand total of three eggs, it was part of my introduction into the fascinating world of birds.

Today the law regarding the protection of wild birds is totally different from when I was a child and for readers of my little book, I would like to make one thing very clear: I trained as a bird ringer and nest recorder under licence from The British Trust for Ornithology. My tuition was received from experts in their field, and it took me over five years to gain my permit and the ability to work unsupervised. It is illegal to intentionally kill or injure any wild bird or take, damage or destroy the nests of wild birds or their eggs.

Later, in my early teens, I would 'borrow' my father's expensive binoculars and I remember the excitement at watching, from my parents' bedroom window, green woodpeckers feeding on ant hills. I also remember well the delight at identifying, for the first-time, species such as goldcrest, coal tit, and dipper, to name but a few. In fact, I kept immaculate records of all the species I saw, including time, location and dates. I was hooked by now, it was unbelievable - the magical world of birds had taken over my young life and has stayed with me this past fifty years.

My father is a fanatical homing pigeon man. He has been all his life. Now almost ninety years of age, his birds are still the spark in his eyes. He would use his binoculars to scan the distant horizons on race day as he awaited the homecoming of his beloved birds. I can still hear him calling, whistling and shaking the corn tin as the newly-arrived pigeons circled the loft. I did have an early interest in this all-consuming hobby but eventually, it was the wild birds and natural history that captivated my imagination.

When I was still a teenager, it was my mother who fuelled my passion further when she would spend her hard-earned cash on buying me some of the best bird identification guides we could afford. A trip to WHSmith in Pontypool would ultimately result in a gift of another book, all of which I treasure to this day.

While still at school, my interest was fuelled by the unequalled enthusiasm and dedication to birds of my old school master and later, very good friend, the late Percy (PFJ) Playford. It was Percy, an expert on pied flycatchers, who taught me that patience and dedication were the only way to study your bird. He was and still is a great source of inspiration to me. Percy educated me in the basics of bird ringing which remains an important part of my study today. These days, I continue under the guidance of Dr. Stephanie Tyler, one of the most hardworking, dedicated and knowledgeable ornithologists I know. Stephanie's main interests lie in the study of dippers and grey wagtails. So, as you can see, when the relaxing hobby of bird watching is simply not enough, most ornithologists take their love of birds a step further. This can happen in several ways, but many choose to spend their time dedicated to a single species or related group of birds. My obsession is with the whinchat and its relative, the stonechat, closely followed by the dipper and the pied flycatcher. My fondness for the latter two species is a direct result of the infectious nature of working in the field with inspiring individuals.

I decided to try and write this book many years ago and it's been a long time coming. I always wanted it to be read, not solely as a reference work but also for interest's sake, by the general bird lover and ornithologists alike. It is full of local references such as place names, especially in the diary extracts, so the local reader with a generally curious mind may consider my little book worth a read.

Obsession

It's true to say that I am more than fond of the whinchat. My involvement with it has given me so many memories, so many sad and emotional times and some very exciting and wonderful times. My name, at least on a local level, is now associated with the whinchat and vice versa. I remain obsessed with this jewel of a bird which is such a huge part of my life. I yearn for its return each spring and still wonder at seeing the first arrivals and finding their hidden secrets in the form of their nests . . . even though I have discovered over 2,000 of them to date. I have gathered information that you won't easily find in books already published and all the information you read here was collected by me and not researched. I don't disagree that so much is known and published about almost every common bird species on the planet, but my study is personal, intimate even.

Why the Whinchat?

I have often been asked: Why the whinchat in particular?

One key memory that contributed to my eventual love affair with the whinchat comes from when I was still in my teens and a rookie bird watcher and nest recorder. In those days, lifelong friend and all-round naturalist Steve Williams and I used to find nests for our then school master, the late P.F.J. Playford (Percy) for him to ultimately ring the chicks in the nest. Steve and I were undergoing early training to become bird ringers ourselves. Having discovered several whinchat nests on the local hillside, we would monitor them before calling Percy to come and ring the broods. One memorable occasion, way back in the late 1970s, one of the young whinchats we ringed that summer was discovered in Portugal, on its way south on summer migration just a couple of months later. It was so exciting to think that such a small bird could achieve such a journey while so young. A lifelong interest was born in me.

Already fond of this little bird generally, I had taken up bird ringing again in my early thirties, after a period of life-changing events. I got married, bought a house and had children. Still, of course, with a passion for natural history in general, I was to climb the hill onto Garn Clochdy which was the view from my home on the opposite side of the valley in the village of Cwmavon. Whinchats were numerous there then but not so common as to lessen my interest in them. I found them fascinating. I found the habitat, the open landscape and the heather moorland equally as pleasing. In those days, the whinchat was under-studied. My peers in the world of ornithology had studied, at great depth, birds such as the dipper and the pied flycatcher and I was determined to achieve the same goals with a species of my own. I pursued my chosen subject with an all-consuming desire to find out as much as I could about them. This soon turned into an obsession.

'Obsessed' or 'downright stupid' is how I've been described on at least one occasion. I was a dedicated amateur footballer all my young life but there was never any conflict with my birding interests because the season for both passions seldom crossed. But, however fit I kept myself, injury was always a possibility in my sport and when I tore the ligaments in my left leg, that became a reality. I was very frustrated at this injury and devastated that I might miss the beginning of the Whinchat breeding season. I missed very few matches at the end of the football season but knew the birds would be nesting and I couldn't walk, particularly across boulder-strewn and tussock-covered terrain on the mountainside . . . or could I? My leg was still in a plaster cast and I needed two crutches, plus of course, I couldn't drive the car. This is where my brother stepped into the breach. I stood a better chance of finding nests on my own and I persuaded him to drive me and wait in the car while yours truly wandered off into the semi-wilderness on crutches. From the vantage point of the car pull-in, he could observe me most of the time, but I took huge risks, at one point clambering over rocky outcrops and larger boulders out of sight. I got around places where a fully-fit person would have struggled but I survived. My study remained complete that summer and I missed very little. A few weeks later, minus the leg plaster, I continued with a limp for the rest of the summer.

Despite being fit - I was oh so very fit in those early days and covering many kilometres every day - it took its toll on my mental and physical wellbeing. At the end of June each year, and after a gruelling schedule on most days during that key month, fatigue would finally catch up with me and stop me in my tracks. It was then that I had no choice but to take it easy for a few days and recharge my batteries for another,

less manic assault in July. There is much less activity among hill birds in July but some second or replacement clutches and broods can still be found. I would still have to cover the same ground as I did the previous month, or I wouldn't be happy and I'd feel my study was incomplete. My wife and children barely saw me for the whole of June and July every year.

Since the early days, I have written about whinchats, given illustrated talks and lent my information to other authors. I have longed to share my study and its results with people, especially close friends, and have gladly enjoyed the company of certain individuals: Dave Lock, a splendid photographer of natural history, and fellow ornithologist and memory maker Mark Lawrence, both kindred spirits. It is, however, here that I can admit that I work better alone. I can 'lose' a day in the hills in sheer concentration when tracking my bird.

I must mention, though, one more unusual companion in the form of my dog - a collie named Heather. I have had the pleasure of knowing many dogs throughout my life and each has been loved unconditionally with their own special traits. But the memories of my time with Heather, my birding companion, are etched into my soul. Her temperament, obedience and loyalty were second to none. She was my confidante when things went wrong and it seemed like both man and dog shared a zest for life and learning. She understood me and I her and I could tell all she wanted to do was please. She was calm and never got over-excited while we worked so as not to frighten the creatures that lived in the environment that was the study area. She stayed at a distance when told but loved to inspect the brood of a pair of whinchats as I held them for ringing. The most amusing thing was that she readily hid under my camouflage netting with me while I observed the birds for as long as it took. She would comb the berries off the bilberry bushes and drink from puddles and streams and go again energetically.

I vehemently don't recommend you let dogs off the lead on the open hillside in the bird breeding season and when there are lambs about. But I knew my dog, and sheep were not a problem, while my super-intelligent companion only followed in my footsteps which were so very carefully chosen through the vegetation. She was so patient and seemed to know exactly what I wanted to do without any training.

Whinchat Ridge

Heather was with me until she was fifteen and suffered a little with arthritis and to a lesser degree, sight and hearing issues. She truly was one in a million.

As I write this in my 66th year, I wonder at my own physical achievements and while I get older, the numbers of my bird get fewer. It's all natural evolution, I guess. Doesn't say I have to like it though, does it?

Meet the Whinchat

The whinchat is a small sparrow-sized bird, often overlooked and fussy about its choice of habitat. It is a summer migrant, arriving in Britain in mid-April, and usually departing by the end of September, rather like the swallow. Also like the swallow and other summer travellers, it has been proven to return to its place of birth more often than not. That's many kilometres of migration each year, around 6,000 kilometres, in fact, and involves crossing the Sahara Desert. The whinchat winters in mid and south-Eastern Africa, in dry scrubby areas of the savannah. The migration has a broad front and also includes the Mediterranean area.

On average, the whinchat arrives back in its breeding grounds in the third week of April with a steady flow of birds into the first week of May. Any March sightings are debatable and very unlikely. There is a definite movement away from the hillside breeding grounds from as early as the end of June and early July (despite some birds still nesting) when individuals and family groups of whinchat are recorded at localities such as Llandegfedd Reservoir and various inland farmland sites throughout the county. The movement of passage off the mountains can, however, continue through August and September and even linger into early October, although by then migration has long been under way. This is strongly apparent by the presence of whinchats along the Gwent coast throughout September and October, with occasional November records (debatable, in my view)[1]. There have been several historical records of birds on the coast during the winter months, such as 3rd January 1966, 6th December 1970, November-end of year 1982, and December 1992.[2]

---

[1] The only explanations for the winter records, in my opinion, is mis-identification or the observation of birds not fit enough to migrate.

[2] See the full Gwent Bird Report on P137

The Habitat of the Study Area

Having arrived in its British breeding grounds, which are primarily in the uplands of the north and west of the country, the whinchat sets about establishing its breeding territories.

The moorland edges and the hillsides, where there are deep gullies and undulating land to give shelter and adequate nesting sites, are the favourite haunts of the whinchat, especially where the vegetation type includes bilberry, bracken and heather. Bracken is often associated with the whinchat and vice versa. The whinchat also benefited initially from the planting of coniferous forests in the uplands, but the local populations were prone to crash as the trees grew larger and relinquished any benefits they once held for the chats as suitable breeding habitat.

Whinchat Ridge

Although the invasive species known as bracken covers vast areas of the study area, much of the undergrowth is made up of dwarf heathland plants such as heather or ling, bilberry or whinberry, crowberry, cross-leaved heath and cowberry. There is a sprinkling of small trees with hawthorn and rowan being well represented. These two species of slow-growing trees are spread by the birds and mammals as the berry seeds pass though their digestive systems after eating. Trees nowadays don't have much chance of getting established because of the grazing regime that's in place. The grazing of livestock on the mountainside is a relatively natural way to conserve and manage a habitat which was largely man-made anyway. But the need to manage is now more important than ever because such specialised species of birds and other wildlife have evolved to depend on it.

Although wildflowers are plentiful, they are probably limited in variety. Some of the bog-loving plants are interesting, with orchids, sundews and the aptly named bog asphodel present, albeit locally.

While some habitat management goes on at the hands of man, I am not totally a fan of the methods, particularly the timing of the operations. Bracken spraying, for instance, is not effective in the long run and the fact that the chemical is administered while the birds are still nesting is something that should be outlawed. Heather burning too, in my opinion, has its problems. It has a season for legal, controlled fires but the seasons change year on year and it's no good sticking to 'the book' when, say, the weather is unseasonably balmy for the time of year and the burn is disturbing the wildlife at the very least. To manage or not to manage, that is the question.

Bracken is often the villain of the piece but can be very important to some species as nesting sites, song perches and providing cover from the elements. Gorse too gets singled out by land managers but is a very important plant species for the likes of the Dartford warbler and linnet.

Heather is one of the most important plants on the mountain side. It helps maintain a healthy population of red grouse. The grouse relies on different stages of the plant's growth for elements of its lifestyle - tall plants to nest and take cover in and younger heather to feed on. Further down on the hillside, heather mixes with other shrub varieties, important for even more diversity. Most ground-nesting songbirds nest in or under the cover of it. Linnets and Dartford warblers have nested in tall, older specimens of it when their preferred gorse is not present. Bees and butterflies swarm to the plant's flowering heads later in the summer. And of course, we humans marvel at the blooms when seen in large quantities along the moorland tracks when we are out walking. But heather alone does not make a perfect habitat for wildlife. A mix of dwarf-like shrubs is ideal, but heather gets a lot of time and attention from land management teams. But we should look at the bigger picture in more detail to create a habitat which is more diverse.

The majority of the heather grows on the tops of the hill where most bracken is currently absent. On the mountain tops, you can expect to see red grouse, skylark and meadow pipits. Lower down on the hillside, the diversity is greater when those species are joined by linnet, reed bunting, yellow hammer, tree pipit and whitethroat, to name but a few. It is here that the cuckoo takes advantage of the scattered trees in which it perches and calls while closely observing the local pipit population. Willow warblers too have adapted to the hillside environment, taking a liking for the scrubby plants, particularly bilberry and bracken, that provide cover and nesting sites. This, I believe, is a result of woodlands and forest edges becoming too dense, perhaps because of under-management. This scenario has also contributed to the loss of typical woodland species such as the garden Warbler and others in the district. All of the mountains within the study area – the Blorenge, Mynydd Garn Clochdy and Mynydd y Garn Fawr - are interlinked and are part of the same ridge. All three have their fair share of damp areas and bracken strongholds, and good mixes of dwarf moorland shrubs can still be found at all sites. There are also areas of stony ground, mainly sandstone but limestone in some places. The peaks of all three mountains are boulder-strewn, and this, as well as open, well-grazed grassland, is where the migrant Wheatear prefers to live. Wheatears arrive in March and can still be seen passing through hilly country in November.

I can't go on enough about the importance of bilberry, locally known as whinberry, as a food source and as protection from the elements and predators. But most of all as nesting sites. It affords the greatest density among all the common hillside shrubs and is a firm favourite with ground-nesting birds. In some localities, like other plants, it is struggling with the more mature bracken stands but by and large, bracken doesn't reach its full potential until the first broods are reaching maturity in the nest, making bracken a timely asset when needed most as extra cover for the newly emerging fledglings.

Large tracts of bilberry have been lost over the years and it can be prone to problems such as diseases, heavy frosts and even abnormal moth infestation. Very often the bilberry will be hardy enough to withstand such attacks, but in some instances it has succumbed and the plant is missing from some localities where it was previously abundant. It is a very important shrub species, and its vulnerability should not be underestimated.

In the late summer when the fruit of the bilberry is readily available, hillside birds thrive on a supplement of the delicious berries, and some will feed them to the young birds that are still in the later nests. Woodland and other species of bird, such as starlings, thrushes and woodpigeons that are not generally associated with the mountainside, also make the most of this free harvest. And of course, people come in their cars and park themselves and their vehicles for many back-breaking hours gathering the same fruit for their own consumption.

The Breeding Cycle

Courtship, nest-building, egg laying and incubation.

Soon after arriving in this country, around the beginning of May, the male whinchat can be heard singing to establish his rights to his chosen territory, attract a mate and declare his intentions to other males in the area[3]. It is at this time that disputes occur over territorial boundaries and the choice of the available females. It is a period of much activity among the birds with high-speed chases and verbal exchanges being the order of the day. The females seem to have a very laid-back approach during this demonstration of masculinity by the flamboyant males. I have witnessed up to three males in hot pursuit of a solitary female as they all 'flew like the wind' low over the vegetation, totally oblivious to anything or anyone that may be watching. Overall, though, any disputes are relatively minor affairs and are soon resolved.

Male interaction is interesting. At the pre-nest building stage, demonstrations of dominance are common but I have many records from the incubation period where individuals have been joined by an 'outsider'. The owner of the territory shows no signs of the aggression or urgency shown in the initial stages of courtship. These males would be perched no more than a few feet apart, both silent, motionless and seemingly unperturbed by each other's presence. This relaxed attitude can be upheld for a duration of many minutes. Quite why this level of tolerance is shown is, as yet, unexplained.

---

[3] See Whinchat Song

When nest building, the female is watched over by the ever-attentive male and there is still a certain degree of confrontation among the birds. However, within a few days the hen whinchat will have all but completed her nest and hidden it away under a bilberry or heather bush. Many nest sites include bracken or indeed a mixture of several types of vegetation typical of the habitat afforded in such upland regions in this part of Wales. The nest is built on or near the ground, occasionally up to six inches or so in a small mound of vegetation such as an old moss-covered ant hill or grass tussock. Some nests can be of a rather open nature, like a robin might construct in a bank for example. But most are so incredibly well hidden, it's a wonder they are ever found.

The nest itself is initially constructed with relatively larger pieces of materials such as dead bracken parts, soft rushes, and thicker sections of dry grasses as well as occasional moss and sheep wool. Thereafter finer materials are woven into a neat tight cup. This consists of mainly fine grasses and is often lined with horsehair or, in the case of the study area, sheep wool fibres.

Once the nest is completed, the female whinchat will start to lay the pale green-blue eggs which are more blue than green and, very often, are lightly speckled with brown on the larger end. These eggs can vary slightly in shape and colour but only under very close inspection will this be noticed.

One egg will be deposited in the nest cup every day until the full clutch is laid. There are normally between five and seven eggs in a typical first clutch with second or replacement clutches averaging four. After the last egg is laid, rarely before, the female alone will start the process of incubation which last around two weeks.[4] It has been recorded that larger clutch sizes and ultimately bigger brood sizes result if the weather and therefore the food supply to the breeding females is plentiful. Usually, a warm and relatively dry May will result in the hen being in a favourable condition and

---

[4] 13 days

more eggs are produced. For example, in such mild springs, the number of nests containing seven eggs increases dramatically.

Certainly, the opposite has been proven, and even though the following month has been perfect, the overall success rate of the whinchat in such a season has been poor, largely due to a cold, damp May. So ideally the species needs fair weather in May and June. Unfortunately, in recent years at least, either one month or the other has been disappointing regarding the weather. At the time of writing this, the whinchat seems to be struggling to recover after several poor summers in the hills.

Female Adding Material to Nest When a Clutch of Eggs Has Already Been Started

I had always assumed that the female whinchat finishes building her nest before going on to lay one egg per day until a full clutch of around 4-7 eggs is achieved. Having found hundreds of nests over the years, I have regularly observed the female whinchat nest-building prior to laying the first eggs. However, during one breeding season, I witnessed two separate cases of female birds which I presumed were in the process of finishing their nests ready for egg laying. In both instances, the birds were carrying noticeable amounts of material such as sheep's wool or a small feather. The nests were found in the usual manner and in each case and to my surprise, two eggs had already been laid. I have thought about this, and although I have not observed this behaviour before or since, I believe that these actions by the female Whinchat may be more common than has been recorded. I believe there are several reasons for this.

One could be that, when a bird is nest-building, I may choose not to find the nest during this time to limit the risk of desertion by the birds. Each pair behaves differently, and I assess each bird accordingly to determine any risk. I then return when a clutch of eggs has been laid. Obviously when the female was laying her eggs, one every day, she could have added further nest material periodically, unobserved by me. This could also happen even when a nest was found originally with young or a full clutch, for it would be unlikely that I would return to that site for at least a week and therefore could easily miss more material being added to a nest. So these actions may be more common or even the norm, even though it took many years and a great deal of close observation before this small but interesting fact was discovered. Below are the actual nest histories concerned with the notes above.

NEST 01-2000 Above the old Inn, Lower Tumble, Blorenge Mountain.

At ground level, under bilberry and moss mound.

21 May	*Female nest building, adding substantial number of wool fibres to a nest containing two eggs! Both male and female being pestered by local stonechat pair. Female whinchat in particular, having trouble getting back to nest.*
29 May	*Female on the nest.*
08 June	*Female on the nest. Sitting very tight.*
12 June	*Female on the nest so tight I could almost touch her! Brooding chicks.*
18 June	*Five out of seven chicks ringed and almost ready to leave the nest. Successful. Chick ring numbers: P460046-50 (5/7).*

NEST 33-2000 Mynydd Garn Clochdy, Cwmavon.

Nest under a bilberry bush at ground level.

07 June	*Female adding lining to nest containing two eggs already.*
10 June	*Full clutch of five eggs.*
23 June	*Young hatching*

28 June Ringed the four chicks that hatched and trapped both parent birds.
30 June All OK at this site. Successful.

During incubation the female will spend more and more time on the nest as the hatching time for her eggs approaches. Early in the incubation period it's easy to observe the hen off the nest in order to follow her back again so that the nest can be located, and its contents inspected and recorded. Later during the incubation period, this becomes more difficult and time consuming because the females are not seen off the nest so much. Indeed, it can be a frustrating time for the most patient of observers, when the birds are sitting very tight and even the male whinchat is not so much in evidence. This is a behavioural fact which fascinates me, because it's now we witness the temporary 'disappearance' of the males. Often these same males can be observed in close proximity to the nest and the incubating female. However, there are long periods of time where the males are clearly absent. It's almost as if they have got bored when the hen is on the nest for so long. It's a quiet secret time, a sort of calm before the storm, but experience has shown me that shortly an 'explosion' of life and activity is just around the corner. Very soon the relatively peaceful life of the human nest recorder will become the manic life of a bird ringer!

The Young In The Nest

Leaving the nest, fledging and pre-migration.

The young whinchat is born blind, (eyes open around the fourth day), naked and extremely vulnerable. During these early days of new life, the female alone will spend a great deal of her time brooding the chicks while the male brings snippets of food to the nest. It is probable that at least some of these offerings end up sustaining the female during her long vigils protecting her offspring. I have never witnessed a male taking food to feed its mate at any other stage during the nesting period, unlike species such as the pied flycatcher which often indulges in this activity when the female is on eggs. I believe if this does occur with the whinchat, then it is very rare, especially when the hen is incubating.

As the days pass, the female will spend more and more time away from the nest in search of food which includes small earthworms, insects and their lava, beetles, bees, moths and, later in the season, the fruit of the bilberry shrub which is plentiful in the study area but not until July when the second and replacement broods are in the nest.

When leaving the nest on one of her feeding forays, the female is usually joined by her mate. Immediately after leaving the site, she flies from perch to perch, gradually moving away from the nest, hopping from each perch to the ground and back in order to feed. I am sure that the hen has a familiar routine regarding the route she takes through the habitat within her territory. At this time, the male whinchat is close by and ever-alert. There is an initial, excited greeting used by whinchats when the birds haven't seen each other for a little time or when re-emphasising a bonding between the pair. This involves a squatting posture and a quivering of wings, almost like a young bird begging or receiving food on an exposed perch, though in this case food is not exchanged by the adult birds.

When the female has had enough of feeding, she may return to the nest in two ways. One is as she left the site, gradually, (associated with a more nervous bird); the other, and one of the more common, is what I call 'the long flight' which is a sudden, straight and direct flight from her final feeding position back to the nest. She will usually spend time preening at some stage before dropping down to the nest to continue incubation of the eggs or brood of the young.

As the days go by, both parent birds now return to the nest with increasing regularity to feed their fast-growing brood of chicks. The female will, however, periodically brood her charges until they are around four days old, especially during periods of cold or wet weather, or in exposed places, both.

Indeed, the young chick is more likely to survive such inclement weather outbreaks due to the warmth and intimate care afforded to them by the attentive brooding female. It is likely the older, un-brooded nestling will perish if adverse weather conditions are prolonged. Food availability when conditions are bad is obviously a major factor at such a testing time.

Within just one week, the chicks are alert and able to move around the nest. I have witnessed individuals who, after taking their fill of food, manoeuvre themselves to a different part of the nest and let a sibling take its place at a prime position at the front of the nest. Faecal sacs, (a membrane which surrounds the baby birds' faeces like a mini sack, allowing clean and easy removal), are taken away at the same time after most visits to the site. This ensures cleanliness and therefore a less smelly nesting site, which in turn becomes a less scent-filled target for any would-be predator, as well as keeping the nest and chicks clean, of course. The adult birds will carry the sac away in their beaks up to a distance of one hundred metres.

Female Taking Food From the Male at the Nest

On 15th June one year, I witnessed a type of 'food pass' at a nest site on Mynydd y Garn Fawr mountainside. At this particular nest site, the young birds had been ringed two days previously, and I had returned to hopefully trap and ring the adults. While under the hide, and observing the site from a safe distance, the female came into view without any food for the chicks. She was perched directly above the nest on a tall bracken frond and looking down on the site in a rather inquisitive manner. This involved her tilting her head from side to side at various angles and staring intensely. Many whinchats, particularly the male birds, will do this directly after a visit by me to the nest, seemingly just to check all is well at the nest and I or a predator am not still lying there in the vegetation. They normally are then contented enough to fly off and continue to search for food.

It was at this point that the male whinchat arrived back at the nest, carrying a beak full of sustenance for the young. He perched right alongside the hen, seemingly intent on entering the nest to feed the waiting occupants. However, the female almost immediately stole the food from the male and aggressively proceeded to peck him in the side of the head. It was as if the female was sending the male back off to find more while she entered the nest, and he immediately did so.

It must be noted that this did not appear to be a voluntary action by the male. The passing of food was one thing, but the show of aggression was another which was interesting to watch.

The full history of the nest involved can be seen below.

Nest No. 13-2000 Mynydd y Garn Fawr

NEST SITE: Under dead bracken shelter.
29ᵗʰ May   Female on 6 eggs, male present.
05ᵗʰ June   6 warm eggs, pair close.
07ᵗʰ June   Young two days old.
13ᵗʰ June   6/6 young ringed. P460273-78. All OK.
15ᵗʰ June   male and female trapped for ringing. Female
recorded taking food from the male in an
aggressive manner.
Male=P460288. Female=P460289.

It is when the chicks are around one week old, that they would be considered for ringing, along with any attempt to trap the adult birds for the same purpose or further detailed processing to collect data[5]. By now the parent-young bird bond is strong enough to withstand a certain amount of disturbance at the nest site through such human activity. I have never witnessed young birds at a whinchat nest being deserted during this period of data collection and indeed desertion at any stage is rare and almost certainly not linked to the activities of my ringing programme.

The defence of the young in the nest is usually limited to loud alarm call notes from the concerned adults. This anxious and vocal alarm is uttered at various distances from a would-be predator as the mature birds try to, at first, lure the danger away. The degree of bravery shown depends on the individual bird and the age of the chicks. I have noticed that some birds are relatively content to keep their distance, calling all the while, until they hear the sound of the frightened youngsters on being held for ringing. It is only then that the adults become braver in their approach and defence. The male Whinchat is often the more 'fear-free' of the sexes and on one or two occasions, I have felt the wings of this little but determined bird on my face, although this is very rare. I used

---

[5] See chapter on Ringing

Steve J Smith

to be able to recognise one male with this habit. He and his mate would nest in the same locality each year and at ringing time, I would have the usual sparring bouts with this bird!

From eight to nine days old, the young chats can actively leave the nest if they are disturbed. This is more likely on hot summer days when the young are well fed and very alert in the warm weather. Between nine and thirteen days old, which is when they leave the nest naturally, they become increasingly prone to 'exploding' the nest in an attempt to escape a potential predator. By using this method, the young birds scatter and distribute themselves at the back of the bush in which the nest is built or out of the front entrance and away to hide under suitable vegetation. Later when the danger has passed, and if all is well at the site, the adult whinchats will come around and feed the young where they are now hiding. I have discovered whole or part broods several feet away from the nest, having recently left the nest prematurely. Individuals will crouch motionless in their hiding place when discovered, relying on their streaked and mottled immature plumage for camouflage. Overall, it's a loss-limitation strategy that is very effective.

If the young birds are not disturbed, they will leave the nest as described above, albeit more calmly, for they cannot fly at this stage. Indeed, they will stay on the ground for days before the lower branches of the vegetation are climbed as they gain strength and confidence. It may be up to another ten days before they are seen in the open and on the tops of the bushes for any length of time, ready to dive under cover at the alarm call of the parent Whinchats.

The adult birds can now divide the responsibility of the fledged brood. Although contact calls keep the family in touch, it can become two separate units. The young whinchat is flying with relative confidence when around one month old and is largely independent and finding food for itself. This is a learning period for the immature birds as they become familiar with their surroundings and accustomed to the dangers in their area.

Whinchat Ridge

The adult birds continue to warn of any possible danger and several families from a given area will group together at this time in what are ultimately pre-migratory parties. These groups will continue to roam their area of birth for some time, and as they fatten up for the long journey ahead, numbers get less and less each day as the birds depart.

Second and Replacement Clutches and Broods

Every breeding season, a certain and variable percentage of whinchat nests are lost to predation, the weather or other factors. Probably, most of those pairs that failed for whatever reason will attempt for the second time to raise a family. Only the loss, due to predation, of one or both adult birds will prevent them from trying, providing the first clutch or brood is lost early enough. Most replacement broods are ready for ringing between the first and third weeks of July, although this is staggered due, of course, to the timing of the individual losses. This is roughly one full calendar month after the first attempts at the beginning of June.

Whinchat Ridge

True second broods are indeed quite a rare occurrence, and even when a pair has been successful early on, it seems to be that most breeding whinchats are content with this and no attempt at raising a second brood is made. Mind you, after a brood successfully leaves the nest, it is very hard, stressful and time-consuming work for the adult birds to lead their young family into independence.

Such second and replacement broods are generally smaller than the first. Second clutches of eggs average around four in comparison with up to six at the first attempt. A fair assumption and a common scenario are that, if a female initially laid six eggs in her first try, she would then go on to lay four in any replacement attempt. Brood sizes will then follow suit, of course. There are always exceptions, however, and I have witnessed pairs that have successfully raised two healthy broods of six.

Steve J Smith

Bigamy Amongst Whinchats

It is very difficult to keep track of the total whinchat population that nests within the study area each summer. At the height of the breeding season, the lives of the whinchat, and, in my case, the totally focused human observer, become extremely hectic. Bigamous behaviour and even polygamy have been recorded in various other species of wild bird but is difficult to prove with small songbirds. A study of the breeding biology of the pied flycatcher, in which I have been involved, showed that it's common for a male flycatcher to have more than one mate. This was proven with the help of intensive ringing schemes, like the one I carry out with the whinchats.

I have found out so much through ringing as many whinchats as possible. Incredibly though, only once have I recorded a male with two females at nests less than one hundred metres apart.

Several years ago, however, I was in touch with some fellow ornithologists from the Nottingham area who had their own, relatively small population study of whinchats, which involved colour ringing individual birds. They indicated bigamy was rather common within their study area. I have concluded that, during the minimal study period, the Nottingham birds, as a small 'fringe' population, often had a surplus male bird and therefore an imbalance between the sexes. But surely in any particular year, this could happen in any size population? All I know is that bigamy is very, very rare in my study area.

Sometimes pair bonding can appear to be weak. Occasionally a pair will seem to have separated after a failed nesting attempt early in the season, and one or two individual birds have been recorded taking another partner for another try. Also, it has been known for a single bird, male or female, to finish raising a brood alone after the loss of their mate to predation or another reason.

The Call of the Whinchat and its Young

The Song of the Male Whinchat

When I first heard the song of the whinchat, I distinctly remember that I thought it was a robin. My experience when dealing with bird song identification could come up with nothing else. But I have since learned that the singing whinchat can not only incorporate some of the sweet and passionate notes of the robin, but the intelligent little migrant can choose to mimic other species as well. Many males in full flow can easily mix the song and calls of other species with its own original song variations.

During one May, a male was regularly recorded as a common whitethroat, due to some marvellous mimicry by the whinchat, while another bird nearby used the first half of the wren's song to kick start its own familiar verbal proclamation. At another site, a male regularly started its song with the first five notes of the chiffchaff. Yet another keen mimic was its neighbour who distinctly sounded the great tit alarm call.

The whinchat is not renowned as a true mimic but over the years, I've heard snippets of tree pipit, robin, starling, (itself an expert mimic), the starting phrases of the chaffinch song, the call of the familiar house sparrow and willow warbler, plus the song of the linnet. Having said all this, the whinchat has a fine song of its own and I now know it off by heart.

The above are simply examples of the capabilities of the male whinchat. Every year I marvel at the vocal skills of my favourite bird as it proudly announces its arrival at the moorland edge in this part of Wales.

The true whinchat song is a rather pleasant warble, not totally unlike the robin, the wheatear or its cousin the stonechat, or indeed reminiscent of all three. At first, its voice does not give the impression that it is loud or powerful. Although, make no mistake, on the open moorland edge its throaty tones can travel a deceptively long distance, especially on a calm still summer's morning or late in the evening and I have heard them through the night while on camping trips in the hills.

The male starts singing on his arrival back on the breeding grounds in April. He arrives a week or so before the female and singing is used as a tool to attract a mate and to ward off any other male intruders to the territory. He continues to sing while the female is on the eggs during May and June, and thereafter less so when the young are in the nest, because he is needed to help feed the constantly hungry youngsters. The male of a pair associated with a replacement clutch later in the season will start singing again when an attempt to repeat the nesting process is initiated. Generally, however, the breeding grounds are devoid of whinchat song as early as the end of June, and certainly from the first week of July, although there can always be exceptions to the rule.

The song is uttered from a prominent perch, which is usually higher than much of the vegetation in the territory. For example, a dry-stone wall, small trees, rock or boulder, bracken or heather bush or fence post. There is a tree pipit-like display flight. This involves a male leaving his song perch and flying almost vertically to a height of several metres, singing all the while, with wings quivering and the brighter parts of his plumage clearly visible for all to see. His position is held in mid-air for a few seconds before the descent is made and he returns to a suitable perch again. I believe it to be associated with the more colourful, flamboyant and sometimes more dominant male, although all will be capable of it. Such song and display demonstrations, while uncommon to come across, are a joy to behold for the observer and the Whinchat seems to enjoy it too!

The tone of the whinchat call varies depending on the time of season and the current circumstances of any given individual bird or pair of birds. As the anxiety level rises with the increasing bonding time, both contact and alarm calls can become more intense in volume and speed of delivery. I can usually tell the stage of the breeding cycle a pair of Whinchats are at by merely assessing the call. Below are some examples described to the best of my ability.

STAGE	TYPE OF CALL AND NOTES
Arrival of the males	*Generally, no calling heard.*
Courtship and pair Bonding	*Very little calling. Only male song. Some gentle alarm can be forthcoming if a bird is surprised when nest building or a predator is noticed.*
Female on egg (early stages)	*Male will call the female off the nest, and she leaves without much persuasion at this stage. A piping call note 'phew' can be heard.*
Female on eggs (later)	*The female will be sitting much tighter during this stage of incubation, and the call of the male becomes more urgent and slightly louder, depending on the closeness and seriousness of the threat.*

Pair with young (newborn)	*Female will brood for long periods during this period and the parental response will be as above. However, at this stage, the call note 'phew' may directly be pursued by a 'tick' so the sound becomes 'phew-tick', and repeated.*
Medium and large chicks in nest	*Both parents are now active lookouts around the nest area. The calls are as above but intensified. The adults are louder as they become more agitated. The call now becomes- 'phew-tick, phew-tick' continuously. Sometimes a loud 'tack' is heard.*
Pair with fledged young	*The alarm is further intensified. By now, the calls of the adult birds are at their loudest and most urgent. The calls are as previously described with the parent birds at their bravest and most concerning. The calls are a signal for the young to lie low while danger is in the area. During this period, the young become vocal also, but only make further contact when the threat has passed. This contact and food acceptance call is a deep 'nasal' churring, uttered from deep within the undergrowth.*

I kept records of all my interactions with my birds. The following is an extract from one year's entries when we also had to contend with a Foot and Mouth outbreak. [6]

Diary Extract

22nd April

Amazingly I recorded my first whinchat of the season from my bedroom window. The mountainside where this bird will ultimately settle down to breed is only just over a kilometre away as the crow flies but to see a whinchat outside my house is a first for me.

It has been raining for several days, and as I awoke this morning, there was a fog over our little river valley and a misty rain was falling. At 8am, there was an uncommon sight of three cormorants flying up the Abersychan valley. They skirted the woodland edge and followed the Afon Lwyd river northwards toward Cwmavon.

There appears to have been an overnight influx or 'fall' of small migrant birds. Around fifty or so swallows and martins milled their way around the fields and low over the river which runs about 30 metres from my garden. Some of these hirundines[7] could be seen perching on telegraph wires over the garden as if resting after their long migratory journey. I have often read about such influxes termed as 'falls' but have never witnessed one. Some such 'falls' are spectacular. Thousands of birds, sometimes blown off course, simply turn up in an area, as if by magic overnight. My gathering, though relatively very small, was nevertheless noticeable.

Along the riverbanks, where tall mature beech and oak trees are dominant, willow warblers and chiffchaff were present in unusually high numbers.

---

[7] Songbirds of the swallow family

Later in the morning, after walking my dogs, I returned to the vantage point at my bedroom window, still marvelling at the morning's proceedings. After scanning the horizon and the hedgerows for movement, I became aware of a small bird perched in a Silver Birch tree and silhouetted against a grey sky. I immediately recognised the species from the few clues on offer. Raising my binoculars, I confirmed what I surely already knew. It was a male whinchat! Normally, at this time of year, I would have to search for hours along moorland tracks and the edge of farmland for my first spring sighting of 'my' bird. But here was one, only metres outside my garden and viewed from the house! The bird was temporarily out of its habitat but not far from Mynydd Garn Clochdy, which is the hill which lies at the top of my lane via a narrow-wooded valley. It just added to the 'mystery' of the morning. Racing outside for a better view, I followed the lone migrant down our lane, where it perched once more, this time at the top of a lane-side ash tree, before it took flight once more over some riverside fields. What a start to the whinchat season for me! They were home. Let the game commence.

26th April

It was a bright afternoon and after a spell at work, I headed for the hills. I arrived on the scenic Llanover Lane, Blaenavon, in a mixed mood which can only be described as bordering on optimism. Traditionally in April I would be excited about the possibility of my first whinchat sighting of the year after their spring migration from Africa and I'd be searching the moorland for the first bird. However, the continuing foot and mouth crisis has limited me to walking the tarmac surface of the lane only, thereby reducing the chance of witnessing my bird's first spring appearance in its usual habitat - though of course I spotted one close to my house only a few days ago. All this obsession has so far been in vain.

I parked the van outside the cattle grid which is on the outskirts of Blaenavon and borders the open common and whinchat country. I made my way through the small gate to the side of the grid, disinfecting my footware as I proceeded. This sterilised green matting, heavily soaked in a liquid chemical, is supposed to limit the possibility of me and other members of the public and their dogs, carrying and spreading the virus onto the moor and surrounding countryside. People are allowed to walk, drive, cycle etc along the tarmac, but treading on the common and even the grass verges of the lane is strictly prohibited. For the purposes of the public, this is most acceptable. However, for the likes of me, this scenario is both extremely frustrating and unproductive as far as my study is concerned. Though I guess it's better than nothing.

Up until recently and for several months now, I have not done so much as this. I have fully respected the farmers' plight and stayed away, but for someone who lives and breathes this wild place and the wildlife that lives there, to have no access feels like a type of imprisonment. My study has been ongoing for many years and will probably be a lifelong one. I can't begin to explain how deeply it hurts to be restricted so.

3rd June

Weather report: AM. rain showers heavy at times. The strong winds of yesterday have died down a little. PM. A cool afternoon but, although a bit brighter, there is still plenty of cloud cover. Incredibly there are reports of snow further north, and it is said to be the coldest start to June on record.

At 14.00 hours I arrived on Llanover Lane, Blaenavon. This mountain lane is an ideal boundary, separating Garn Fawr to the north and Garn Clochdy to the south. I was lucky that I didn't have too much trouble in re-finding all four whinchat nests I'd found before, despite the fact that they were not 'marked' properly on the day I originally found them. Normally for me, a suitable marker in the form of a piece of knitting wool is tied on vegetation near the nest for easier re-location and it is at times like this when I realise the value of using this method. All four nests contained young between one and two days old. It is typical that the young of first broods hatch around the first week of June, but the chicks will require special care during such inclement weather conditions. The hen whinchat must undoubtedly be brooding a lot to prevent her young from chilling.

Moving toward Garn Clochdy, above Cwmavon, I was aware that meadow pipits were very active in the area. Adult pipits were alarm calling almost continuously at my presence as they shepherded their recently-fledged youngsters through the damp undergrowth to safety. These juvenile birds took off almost from under my feet before disappearing into the undergrowth a couple of yards away. I continued my journey into whinchat country and I was again made aware of how successful the meadow pipit is as a species.

Later, while under the hide observing another pair of whinchat, I had a fine view of a fox which stared back in my direction with its head and shoulders above the bracken. It was now that the whinchat pair joined forces with some anxious pipits and mobbed the lone predator as it trotted off though the moorland shrubbery. I suspect that the fox will prey on ground-nesting birds, and I believe that this can result in destruction of the nest, eggs and young, particularly in the case of the smaller species like the chats, pipits and larks.

After the fox had left the scene, I continued to watch my pair of whinchats in the hope of finding their nest. It was then that a curious thing happened. Before the female could return to the site, the male bird visited the nest, thus giving me the impression that there were young in there. When I finally located and checked the contents of the nest, I found six eggs. Why the male whinchat went to the nest containing eggs and no female is of interest to me. Perhaps it was to check all was OK after the retreat of the fox, or were the eggs due to hatch? I have noticed many times before that the male birds will often be first back to the nest after a disturbance as if to check the site and reassure a nervous female. I have also suspected that an attentive male will somehow sense when a clutch of eggs is due to hatch and make more frequent visits to the nest at this time.

Walking on a little further, I stopped, as I frequently do, to marvel at my surroundings. Garn Clochdy is a fantastic place of folk law and legend, a place of beauty and of childhood memories. It's a haven for flora and fauna and in my opinion deserves special protected status like the neighbouring Blorenge.

Just then, another pair of whinchat caught my eye. These birds caused me to smile in pure fascination. While the female busied herself carrying nest material, the male bird followed her around with an offering of food. The hen energetically continued to search the ground for nesting material and to my amazement, she finally went down into the undergrowth and her nest, carrying some snowy white sheep wool fibres . . . by now the male had had enough of being ignored and devoured the food!

I went on to observe a recently-fledged family of stonechat which I had had the pleasure of ringing and monitoring previously. Always good to witness such success.

I checked a few more whinchat nests on the way back to my van parked at Llanover Road. It was here that I discovered another new nest, much to the amazement of a passer-by, an elderly Blaenavon gentleman who, on being shown the nest containing six eggs, exclaimed, 'How on earth do you find such well-hidden nests?' 'Experience,' I replied. But deep down, I once again realised just how privileged and plain lucky I am.

29th June

It was fine weather for a change as I parked my van near the historic Forge Row in the village of Cwmavon. My ascent toward Garn Clochdy and the open moorland first takes me through a mature larch plantation, where there are nesting sparrowhawks, and past the hill farmstead where I take the concrete road to the hill. This track normally allows vehicular access to the maintenance crews that service the tele-mast that stands proud on the edge of the moor. Ravens love to nest near the top of this mast from where they can survey the landscape for kilometres. Apart from the local farmers, no one else is allowed access with a motor vehicle.

This time of the season has its drawbacks - finding second or replacement clutches or broods can be difficult and frustrating for the human observer. Locating pairs of whinchats for watching back to the nest becomes harder when many other birds already have fledged young in the area. Many of the other species nesting on the hill are extremely wary of my presence and it's more difficult than normal to hide without being discovered. They can give the game away by alerting the very birds that you have come to watch. This can lead to much confusion and it is then I need to be even more patient and stealthy.

At seven o'clock this evening, however, I was ready to trudge off the mountain side and in the mood to 'sulk for Wales', with nothing going my way! I decided this was not the attitude of a responsible ornithologist and, for some reason, fresh optimism duly crept in. It's digging deep at times like this that makes all the difference in achieving the results you want from your study.

Eventually, while watching a family party of whinchats communicating loudly among themselves, a lone and rather quiet male bird became visible in the field of view through my binoculars. This meant that there may be a female whinchat on a nest somewhere and my spirit was lifted by the thought of the challenge of finding out more. Fifteen minutes later and a nest containing five sky blue eggs was discovered, hidden deep within the tall bracken, and I congratulated myself on my field craft skills when all had seemed lost - at least on that day.

This scenario never ceases to amaze me. This, a traditional site for nesting whinchats, had been checked out by me on several occasions this very season, and even though I suspected I would eventually find a nest here, I was just about to give up hope.

This brings me to question the accuracy of field survey work relating to bird numbers. Although its value should not be totally dismissed, two or three site visits through a given survey area cannot give the recorder a true picture of the bird population that lives there. I can recall leading a good friend of mine through my Garn Clochdy study area to show him the whinchats that resided there. We recorded around six pairs that day during quite a thorough search. My companion questioned me, light-heartedly, as to the whereabouts of all the whinchats I'd boasted about during our previous conversations. We left the moor that day with my explanations ringing in his ears. That year, nearly fifty pairs (one hundred whinchats), graced Garn Clochdy, and all those birds would have been present the day my friend and I had walked through!

On the return journey back down the hill this evening, I was lucky enough to locate yet another pair of whinchats. Their nest contained six eggs. So, I had turned pessimism into optimism and reaped the reward of the extra effort. What a bonus!

1st July

The weather's been fine for two days now, not very warm, however, but it's so much better than anything we had during the whole of June! The wettest June on record, they say, while last June had set the previous record!

I noticed a profusion of flying insects today, more than I've seen all summer so far. This is good news for the birds and the later broods.

Whinchat Ridge

I have arranged to meet my friend, Mark Lawrence, at his study site overlooking Crickhowell, but first I must make a visit to Garn Clochdy via Llanover Road.

Back in June, I had recorded a male whinchat in full song at a time when, all around him, other whinchats were hard at work feeding their broods. I had made a mental note of this and today is the day I followed up my hunch of a possible nest. I was soon congratulating myself when, within fifteen minutes, I had located a nest here containing five lovely sky-blue eggs. I also noticed that the male bird is carrying a ring, like around 75% of the whinchats in the study area right now.

It was now I decided to check on the other side of the lane, which is the edge of Mynydd-y Garn Fawr, where I checked another whinchat nest that contained five eggs also.

A quick visit to the nest of Wales's first breeding Dartford warblers revealed that all was fine at this secret site.

Away now for Blaenonneu with its towering panoramic views, via the Heads of the Valley road and Garnlydan. I arrived at 4.30pm and it didn't take me long to locate Mark's van and the chocolate-munching individual who drives it! There's hardly time for a healthy diet this time of year and we favour pocket snacks that can be eaten any time and on the move. Totally unhealthy but we both rely on short bursts of energy at frequent intervals during the day.

Greetings and data updates exchanged, we were soon off over open areas of grassy well-grazed common land to a lovely horseshoe-shaped low hill. Our reason for this was to investigate a pair of whinchat and hopefully trap the adult birds that are present. On route, we saw an adder as it lay motionless at the foot of the little hill. These seemingly listless vipers are slightly worrying. All the books that I have read say that adders will do almost anything to avoid confrontation and that, at the first sign of human presence, they will slither away to find a safe hiding place. My experience is that you can get very close to adders, particularly during periods of cooler weather when they are much more lethargic.

Within fifteen minutes, both adult whinchats had been trapped and all the relevant details recorded. I ringed two broods of meadow pipit for Mark and then he went on to show me a young cuckoo in another pipit nest. The gigantic chick took up the entire nest, appearing to be stuck in the tiny hollow, which was the nest cup, surrounded by bracken.

Just a word about the wonderful views from this site. You have an amazing outlook over the Brecon Beacons National Park, Llangorse Lake and the Sugar Loaf mountain towards Abergavenny.

Such exceptional views go hand in hand with whinchat watching.

7th July

It's traditional for me to watch whinchats on my birthday, and with a bit of luck, locate a new nest or two. After a wonderful day out with the family, I amble up our steep lane through the gate and the mountain wall at Penyrhoel Farm where the slopes of Mynydd Garn Clochdy begin. It's a rough old access track that leads me to the edge of the common which is a prime area of mixed wet and dry heath. It was getting a bit late, and at 7.30 in the evening, I was limited in what I could achieve. However, I watched the whinchats in this area until the sun went down over Coity mountain to the west. Distant farm dogs were barking in the valley below and the light was fading on this place of myth and legend.

Whinchats are active until dark, and it is lighter for longer up on these open hills than down in the Lasgarn Woods which nestle in the cwm (valley) below. These woods are devoid of the late evening rays. During a camping trip in 1996, I heard male whinchats singing during the middle of the night. A sleepless night for me, I recall, a magical memory though, lying beneath the stars in my heaven on earth with the song of sweet angels penetrating the darkness of an otherwise silent night.

Whinchat Ridge

This evening, it was so very cold for the time of year. It's time for reflection in this beautiful place and I became rather sentimental. Another season with the whinchats will be over soon, and the purple heather will be the moorland's parting gift, the finishing flag and summer's end. It was now that my memories of the past collide with the present and even possibilities for the future made an appearance as my mind tried to decipher it all. It will soon be over for another year, but until then, I shall continue with enthusiasm to collect all the information I can from my life study of the chats.

As I descended the hillside, I came back down to earth. I now have fresh concerns over the bird ringing part of my study. There is a lack of rings due to a shortage at the British Trust for Ornithology HQ in Hertfordshire. I would dearly like to ring the young birds in the remaining whinchat nests I have found in the study area. With my usual provider abroad, rather desperately I decided to contact another ringer for help. To my delight, he agreed to help so that the ringing part of my study can continue as planned.

8ᵗʰ July

At 8am, I met my contact Jerry just outside the town of Pontypool to pick up the rings I wanted to continue my study. By 4pm, I had joined my friend, fellow ornithologist and ringer Mark Lawrence on the lower slopes of the Blorenge mountain which affords marvellous views over the Usk valley and lies within the Brecon Beacons National Park and the Blaenavon World Heritage Site.

Our objective was to return to previously-found nests in order to ring the nestlings. Armed with my newly acquired rings, I successfully ringed a brood of stonechats and a brood of whinchat. Both healthy broods of chats wouldn't have waited any longer and they will be leaving the nest very shortly.

At 6pm, Mark and I found ourselves on Mynydd y Garn Fawr to the south of the Blorenge and part of the same ridge.

It's on the edge of the old industrial town of Blaenavon and connects Garn Fawr with Garn Clochdy above my home. The habitat is similar to Garn Clochdy, with a mixed dry-wet heath making for a valuable and diverse habitat, perfect for breeding chats.

Mark and I set a licensed trap and were successful in catching two adult male whinchat from neighbouring nests. Both birds were particularly brown and obviously in moult, a typical scenario found later in the breeding season. We swiftly recorded all data from the measurements of each bird and released them. The faeces of one of the birds showed dark purple, indicating that it had been feeding on bilberries (whinberries) recently, and this time of year, my hands are often stained with the substance as proof of this! The fact that there was a relatively poor crop of the delicious whinberries this summer comes as quite good news in a somewhat selfish sort of way. Less fruit equates to fewer disturbances from people on the moors. I have had birds desert the nest because of berry pickers who can be totally oblivious to the distress calls of a parent bird while focused on picking their beloved fruit. After all, generations of people have participated in harvesting whinberries and it's common to see two or three generations out picking at one time, with the elders passing on their local knowledge. Any disturbance, I believe, is born out of ignorance and not done intentionally. The main problem lies in the fact that the whinchat likes nothing better than to build its nest under a whinberry bush! Also, the human gatherers can spend hours in one location, so simply moving sites periodically would eradicate any problem.

At least it's only the minority of nests that have this to cope with because it's only the replacement broods that are affected and these are relatively few. All the first broods are off the ground and flying by the time the berries are ripe for the picking.

One hour later and Mark had left for home. I raced to Cwmavon village and climbed the concrete access road to the mast and on to Garn Clochdy via the old drovers' route. While making my ascent, I met a Varteg man heading in the same direction. We engaged in conversation and discussed our reasons for being there. He was to help the local hill farmers in the job of gathering sheep, in order they may later be sheared. He showed great interest in my activities also and seemed truly amazed when I showed him a whinchat nest deep in the undergrowth. 'So small and well hidden,' he said. 'How on earth do you....?' The usual thing.

I went on to ring the stonechat brood I had come for. While the young of this species were ready for ringing, the brood of their cousin, the whinchat, was only just hatching, being a typical replacement nest after a loss in June, so I pencilled them in for another visit in about a week's time.

By now, it was getting late, and my last memory of this evening would be the distant sight of the farmers and their helpers silhouetted against the evening sky. Their voices and those of their charges echoed on the otherwise silent moorland landscape.

12th July

Heavy rain and strong winds are once again the order of the day. This makes me anxious for the birds that are still nesting, and for me, this inbuilt urge to be on the moor and among them makes me edgy and irritable.

Suffering from boredom and frustration due to the continuing adverse weather conditions, I left home in the van in a lull in the rainfall. Up on Llanover Road, Blaenavon, it was still blowing a gale as I stepped out onto the moor. It's becoming increasingly common for me to don full waterproof kit including Wellington boots during part of the summer in the hills. Disturbing the nesting birds and, in particular, the ringing of birds is totally off limits during such poor weather conditions. I saw very few small songbirds and noted once again that the presence of a strong wind makes for very poor birdwatching conditions. All the small songsters, the chats included, tend to 'lie-low' and are reluctant to use their usual

prominent perches. Along with this, one's hearing is also greatly impaired so that the alarm calls of the whinchat cannot be heard, even at close quarters. Being able to hear the various alarm and contact calls is a crucial part of my nest-finding techniques. All this adds to the frustration but I still love to be on this mountain among the wildlife.

Leaving Llanover Road, which is no more than a single-track lane linking Blaenavon with Llanover, I drove the few kilometres to the mountainside on the opposite side of the valley known as Coity which overlooks the village of Varteg. There was a slight chance, while the rain stopped, that I may find a late nest or two, or at least gain some clues to their whereabouts so that I could return at a later date. The poor weather conditions, however, continued to thwart my attempts and my frustration grew. I trod gingerly through the undergrowth, in particular bracken, which is at its tallest right now and is chest hight on me at this location.

Though the wind had died down considerably, the only whinchats I recorded were two independent juvenile birds, alone in a sea of bracken tops.

Lower down the hillside, and near my parked van, I saw a rather nice male reed bunting carrying food from the bracken and heather to its nest of chicks in the rushes near the old track side. At this moment, a buzzard called from a small beech woodland on the edge of the moorland.

13th July

Fine weather all day! However, it's still not very warm and there's the ever-present threat of more rain with now familiar cloud cover looming overhead.

During a particularly cruel, cold and wet season, where my Wellington boots are just as much a part of my birding kit as my binoculars, I must still admit that the call of the wild captured my heart as it always does. Despite the stress and the worry of it all (I feel so much for the birds when they struggle), I shall go on studying my beloved whinchats for as long as I am able. Seasons come and seasons go, but individual memories last for ever.

Finally, I arrived on the Blorenge mountain at six o'clock in the evening and immediately re-located whinchat nest number eighty-one. This has been the most whinchat nests I have ever found during a bumper couple of years for the species. However, I know just how vulnerable they can be, especially if these weather patterns continue for any length of time.

Nest eighty-one is a good nest, attended energetically by two parent birds and now containing five, one-week-old chicks, which were perfect for ringing. The nest is neatly tucked away in a whinberry (bilberry) bank and amongst bracken. Within ten minutes, I'd caught both male and female birds here and ringed the brood. This is a typical replacement nest of a pair that I know lost their first brood through predation. I noticed that particularly the male bird was undergoing his pre-migration moult. This puts extra pressure on the adult birds and for them and their late-born youngsters, it's now a race against time, for within eight weeks, they must be ready to leave for Africa. I have on occasions witnessed whinchat nests containing young birds on the very last day of July. That's pushing it!

Most of the early territories in this traditional site are silent and devoid of whinchats now, but small family groups can be observed nomadically wandering the moorland edge, the young birds within these groups growing stronger and more independent by the day.

When juvenile whinchats leave the nest, they can't fly initially, and the responsibility for the brood is often split between the male and female birds. Each adult will take care of roughly half of the newly 'fledged' brood and this could lead them in opposite directions. However, they keep in touch with constant contact calls. The family may not necessarily stay separated for good and may become a single family unit once again when the young can fly, which is between one and two weeks after initially leaving the nest. The reason for such behaviour is to confuse any would-be predator and to increase the odds of survival for at least some of the brood while they are at such a vulnerable stage in their development.

Further searches for late nests along the mountain lane on the lower Blorenge proved to be fruitless. Many whinchats have moved on, with some of the early successes and even some birds from failed attempts already starting their migration, and while their movements may, for the time being, be localised, breeding whinchats from the uplands may be observed in lowland areas from July onwards at the very start of their long outward migration.

14 July

Stepped out onto Garn Clochdy moor at 6.30pm and even the constant threat of further rain could not dampen my urge to be amongst the birds and to feel part of this beautiful and in some ways, mysterious place. I parked the van near Hafod-Wenog Farm on the lower slopes and I headed in the direction of Cwmavon along the old bridle way. I was aiming for a nest I had found previously, and the chicks should now be ready for ringing. When I arrived at the nest on the banks of a small cwm stream, I discovered the young birds to be, thankfully, OK, though a touch on the small side. It seemed to be some time, around three or four minutes, before the adult whinchats arrived on the scene and gave off the characteristic alarm call aimed at me, the intruder. This initially gave me the impression that all was not well at this site. I decided to put off ringing here for a further two days. This I don't mind because it will only give me another excuse to return to this place. I then took great strides out across the moor with its interesting diversity of habitat vegetation including heather, bilberry, crowberry, bracken and damper areas of soft rushes and cross-leaved heath. This vegetation is deep, and step-restricting and makes for tired legs come the end of the day. It was now that I noticed the poor crop of bilberries this year. At this time of the season, woodpigeons and thrushes can gather in relatively large post-breeding season flocks as they arrive in search of the lush, black-purple fruit, and the late broods of whinchat are often supplementary fed on them.

While heading north-west toward Cwmavon, I was drawn to a place where a pair was unfortunate enough to have lost its first brood in June. Initially, the first attempt failed when the young died at two days old. However, there was good news when I ringed a healthy brood of five chicks at the site this time around. I feel privileged to be able to do so at a time in the breeding calendar when all whinchat finds are a bonus. I wished them good luck.

By now the rain was stopping and starting as if to tease and frustrate me and there were ominous black clouds racing in from the west.

The stonechat brood that I ringed near the tele-mast directly above Cwmavon were doing just fine, judging by the alarm calls of the adult birds on my approach.

While checking out two previously found whinchat nests in the area, I was pleasantly surprised to discover another pair showing all the signs of having something to hide, such as a nest containing chicks perhaps. After hiding under camouflage for a little while, I finally located nest number 83 for the year. This was a second brood for this particular pair. I shall return to hopefully ring them on another day. I set off back towards the van, a very happy man with a spring in my step and the calls of the birds ringing in my ears.

Near the gate to Hafod-Wenog Farm and my parked vehicle, an immature cuckoo flew off the moorland fringe, encircled me twice before alighting in a small tree along the old stone wall which leads to the farm, its comparatively gigantic form silhouetted against the evening sky. The loyal and attentive parent birds, in this case a pair of meadow pipits, fed 'their' oversized offspring, oblivious to my presence. It's hard to believe that, at any other time, the pipits regard the cuckoo as an enemy and mob the larger bird when it enters its territory. Also, all the adult cuckoos leave our shores well before any of the young birds are ready for migration. How do the youngsters find their way? The wonders of nature and particularly bird migration were my parting thoughts as I left Garn Clochdy for home.

20th July

A day off work, but with little time to donate to birding with domestic duties taking preference. I found myself yearning for the hills and the Whinchats there.

It was nearly 7pm when I finally pulled up my van at the 'Carn y Gorfydd' car park on the Llanellen lane that takes you to Llanfoist and Llanellen in one direction and climbs the slopes of the Blorenge in the other. The fog was down and visibility was very restricted. This was frustrating, but at least

I was here in this wonderful place at this intriguing time of year.

I turned off the van's engine and stepped outside and the silence was deafening! It was so eerily quiet, I could hear the sheep tearing at the grass while they grazed some distance away. This was such a contrast to the hustle and bustle of June when the hill was full of song and the activity of fledged immature birds following their parent birds around. Eventually, a distant willow warbler could be heard communicating with its recently fledged brood, while a wren too could be heard with its familiar cheeky 'Tick, tick, ticking' alarm call dominating the stillness. Down in the valley below, where a lonely farmstead lies, all was quiet and calm except for the cry of a proud cockerel penetrating the hill fog as if it were but feet away. Any sound, no matter how insignificant, was being amplified by nature's own methods. I walked rather solemnly along the footpath that headed south from the lane and the car park. My stroll revealed to me what I really didn't want to accept, even though I already knew in my heart. The truth was that whinchat nest finding here was over for another summer.

22nd July

It had been raining almost all day, mostly drizzle, but with the occasional heavy shower in the afternoon.

I arrived on the mountain lane between Cwmavon and Blaenavon at six o'clock in the evening with the main aim of getting out of the house to stretch my legs and to exercise my mind. I find the inclement weather and the lack of activity in my life at this present time, all too frustrating and brain-numbingly boring. I find it a bit of a come down and an overall anti-climax when the whinchat breeding season is at or coming to an end and every year a period of adjustment, both mentally and physically, is called for. For the past few months, I have lived and breathed these mountainsides and lost some weight in the process. Passion, obsession, call it what you will.

Unsurprisingly, my simple walk along the tarmac lane turned into an amble on the moor. By now, the rain had eased off but still I was fully clad in waterproof gear, which I had to don more often this summer than during any other I can remember. Before long, I found myself heading for the last remaining whinchat nest and I could not resist a quick visit to check the contents. I found myself greeted by a very attentive pair of adult birds, who were feeding their offspring regularly, despite the poor weather conditions. When I had first discovered this nest, it had contained three eggs in what was a typical late clutch. Two of the eggs have hatched and both chicks, about a week old, and looking good and well fed, are obviously enjoying the attention afforded to them by two determined parents. When the food supply is suppressed due to the weather, a large brood would struggle more than a small brood, as in this case. Also, the fruit of the whinberry bush is available to the later broods, which helps to supplement their normal diet of caterpillars, earthworms and insects.

I felt it safe enough to ring both chicks and this was carried out in double quick time, before I retreated away from the site with feelings of mixed emotions. I had more than likely ringed my last brood and seen my last nest of Whinchats for another year.

On my return journey towards the lane, I recalled the nest site vegetation and the fading yet beautiful colours of summer's end. The autumnal feel that surrounds me so early has been brought on by the dreadful weather we have all endured. The bracken near the nest site, and elsewhere on the moor, is already turning with blackened edges and traces of gold and red. All this, despite the fact that summer still has time to redeem itself and I'm praying for a fair and gentle August to see the birds on their way to a safe migration.

Other species active on the damp hillside this evening were some linnets in noisy, chattering, gregarious family parties and the numerous and highly successful meadow pipit. I also came across a mixed group of stonechat and whinchat near the lane. The young birds from earlier in the season were exploring the terrain with their parents close at hand. I wormed my way under my canvas hide and watched the action from a distance as the sun came out. I imagined that I was again observing the chats as if it were peak season and not the end of one. But instead of the high tension, I was in a more relaxed, calm state of mind. I was already looking forward to next summer and getting close to the birds at the nest once again.

A grasshopper warbler sang its curious song from the now familiar spot in a nearby marsh as the sun went down. It was only then that my mind focused on the eccentric nature of my activity. The sounds of distant motor vehicles, barking dogs and the echoing unintelligible voices of people walking the lane decided to make an appearance in my consciousness. I was so engrossed and obsessed with my passion for the birds that I hadn't noticed life going on around me. My fellow human beings were enjoying their evening walks, unaware that only a short distance away on this largely inaccessible slice of Welsh moorland, lay a lone but not lonely man who was not only generally oblivious to them, but liked it that way.

Life History of a Whinchat

It's not only unusual but extremely rare to have a full life-history of a small songbird. The following notes are an example of a true life-history of a whinchat that I originally ringed as a chick in the nest and, in a few words, document the bird's life...and death.

June **Year One**: **K622865** Male whinchat was born along with five siblings on the hillside at Llanover Lane, Blaenavon.

Year Two: **K622865** returned to Wales as an adult breeding male and nested less than a kilometre away from where he was born the previous year, having undergone a successful migration to Africa and back. He and his mate raised four young together.

Year Three: After another migration, **K622865** returned to Llanover Lane, Blaenavon and again nested amongst the heathland shrubs there, only 200 metres from the previous nest site. He and his mate raised a small brood of three chicks successfully.

August **Year Four**: Sadly, after searching the old nests of sparrowhawks in a Blaenavon forestry plantation less than a kilometre from the moorland habitat, the ring of **K622865** was discovered in the debris there. We concluded that, as the hawk nest was inhabited the year before, that **K622865** was taken as food by the hawk, soon after I had last recorded him.

There you have it, the life history of a small migrating songbird. The few compressed notes above do not truly describe the wonder of it all, or the emotion in finding out the truth.

Finding the nests

The Hidden Secrets

First, some basic yet essential tools when watching whinchats back to the nest. In my opinion, these are binoculars, a piece of camouflaged netting or canvas and a notebook and pen.

While walking a given area which the whinchat is known to inhabit, look for movement on the top of vegetation and listen for their call which will tell you that the birds have seen you and have something to hide. Ideally you will soon locate a pair, and of interest to you initially is the female. If it is late May through to mid-July and the birds are alarming, then you are in the territory of nesting whinchats. Find yourself some high ground, but not so that your body is visible above the skyline, and overlook the site where the nest will probably be hidden. Get comfortable and hide yourself well and do this at a fair distance. The birds then feel safe and think you have departed, and they start to act naturally again. Fixing your field glasses on the female (or the male if he's carrying food), as soon as you possibly can, you then follow her without distraction for as long as it takes. Watch her every movement and lack of movement for up to twenty minutes or so, or whatever the duration, until she's ready to return to the nest. Remember, be prepared because she could decide to return at any moment, and you don't know how long she's been off the nest already. When the bird eventually returns, try and make a mental note of the last perching point as she drops to the nest and 'mark' it visually and continue to visualise it as you approach the nest site. Try and walk to the place without taking your eye off the final perch if you can but take care - in a sea of tall bracken and an uneven boulder-scattered landscape, this can be dangerous to you.

Another and more important thing to remember is always to be careful when approaching a nest site as it is the nature of the bird to build on or near the ground. There may also be nests of other species in the area, so please remain aware of your surroundings and the greater picture relating to what else may be going on around you. I cannot stress enough that it is illegal to disturb wild birds at the nest and should be linked to proper training in field craft, surveying, ringing and licensing in general.

Sometimes repeated attempts are required to be successful but use your discretion here also, so that the birds are not over-stressed, and you end up making an absolute mess of the protective vegetation by trampling the area down. If the nest is proving a little difficult to locate, then move on to another site, maybe to return another day.

On finding a nest, record the contents and, in my case, I tie a tiny piece of knitting wool on a bush nearby to make it easier to re-locate on future visits. Don't make the mistake of thinking you'll remember the site exactly, because you won't once the memory fades. The vegetation around the site will continue to change its appearance almost daily as well as grow taller in many cases.

If the pair has young in the nest, it should be easier to find out their secret, because the parent birds will be making repeated and much more frequent visits to feed the chicks. Otherwise, the procedure is the same - locate, hide, observe, find. Easy when you know how!

There is, of course, a certain variation to this theme. For example, in late May and early June, a sighting of a lone male whinchat in suitable terrain will almost undoubtedly signify that there is an incubating female close by. On your approach, the alarm call of the male bird will be heard as you near the nest. At this stage, the female might vacate the nest so you have to wait and watch for her return. However, if the alarm uttered by the male is of an urgent and continuous nature and the hen whinchat is sitting very tight in the later stages of incubation, then she might not leave the nest at all. She may continue to sit tight until the danger has passed.

The observer has two options here - he or she can either hide and watch to assess the situation or return later.

When observing the female in this situation with a view to finding her nest, her every movement must be scrutinised carefully, for you dare not lose her as she disappears, then reappears in your field of view. Binoculars are fixed continuously on her and disregarding all other distractions around you, it's that 'long flight' that you are waiting excitedly for. Follow her back now and her secret could, with care, be yours.

Sometimes, however, repeated attempts are required to make a discovery.

I would like to say that I have decided to include this chapter to encourage ornithologists and like-minded people who genuinely love birds and mean well. Remember, don't break the law!

Relationships With Other Species

Generally speaking, you will never witness a flock of whinchats. Their arrival at the breeding grounds is usually marked with a solitary male or a few early birds scattering the study area. The only gregarious tendencies shown by this species is when they can sometimes gather in loose family groups in the late summer and the post-breeding season. I have recorded up to forty birds loosely together after a successful breeding season on the moorland. Today, in 2024, you will be lucky to see half a dozen birds together post-breeding, such is their decline. Very often, such groups, which are usually smaller in number, will also include a certain number of stonechats, a close relative of the whinchat. These parties of locally nomadic birds will gradually move away, and I have observed them slowly diminishing in number until all have migrated from the breeding grounds at the start of their long journey to Africa. This can include the largely non-migrant stonechat, which ringing has proved can sometimes migrate, but many birds will stay on the hillside through a mild winter.

Those stonechats which remain on or near their traditional breeding grounds through a mild winter are joined again the following spring by those with migratory tendencies. Many stonechats will have set up territories before the whinchats have arrived, choosing the prime sites, and may have a nest with young in it before all the whinchats have taken up a territory of their own. Therefore, the largely resident stonechat will have the opportunity to raise up two or three broods in any one season, while the whinchat will be lucky to have the time to raise one or two. Realistically there is plenty of room for both species to co-exist.

In the study area, the whinchat used to outnumber the stonechat 5 to 1. Sadly as I write this in July 2024, the opposite is true. However, despite their close relationship during the post-nesting period, the stonechats show a different character during the breeding season. They will not tolerate the whinchats near their nest site and, while the female is sitting on eggs, the male stonechat will spend much of his time chasing off bewildered whinchat and other species such as meadow pipits from his territory. I have on many occasions recorded the relentless 'hounding' of a female whinchat by a male stonechat while all the hen whinchat wants to do is take a well-earned rest off the nest of eggs she has been incubating. There appears to be a general pecking order amongst the small songbirds that inhabit the moorland edge, and this is summarised below. From one to five, the most dominant species are:

Wheatear, stonechat
Whinchat
Skylark, reed bunting
Linnet
Meadow pipit

In its turn, the whinchat can show aggressive behaviour toward all other species close to its own size. These include the meadow pipit, linnet, reed bunting and the larger skylark. I often feel sorry for the gentle meadow pipit because it seems to receive the brunt of intolerance from almost all other species and, due to the fact it's by far the most numerous bird on the hill, it is a key prey species too.

I have witnessed a male whinchat rob a skylark of its recently acquired food item (a small earthworm), while both species fed side by side in a field during the spring arrival period. The larger lark had no intention of putting up a fight for its meal as the newly arrived migrant stole from its mouth! I watched closely as the lark continued to search for more food, as the whinchat hung on to the bigger bird's every movement, presumably waiting for another free handout from its docile provider.

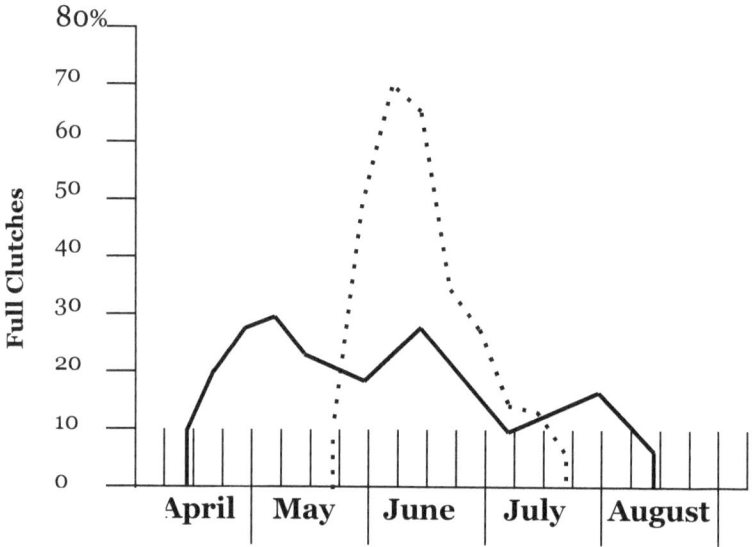

Key:

Stonechat: ———— **Whinchat:** – – – –

The extended breeding season of the stonechat compared with the limited activity of the whinchat.

Other Species

The whinchat shares its summer breeding space with a handful of species of a similar size. The next few paragraphs give an introduction to some of those species that I consider as being typical of the moorland edge. I have not included those that may simply have a habit of passing over from time to time in their quest to reach their favoured feeding areas, such as the wooded hillsides or fields of the valley bottom.

The Stonechat (*saxicola torquata*). About the same size as its close relative, the whinchat, the stonechat shares many of the behavioural characteristics of its cousin as well as its habitat and food requirements. The male stonechat is a beautiful and striking bird when seen at close quarters. It has a jet-black head and throat, which contrasts strongly with its dark red breast and flashes of white on its wings when in flight. The plumage of the female is much duller and she appears mostly brown, at least from a distance. It is a largely resident species, with most breeding pairs within the study area choosing to remain on the hillside or at least in this country during our winter months. Ringing has proven, however, that some stonechats will migrate long distances. As personal examples, two extraordinary ringing recoveries of mine prove this. One was of a week-old chick ringed by me in the Powys mountains and which turned up only months later in North Africa, and a female bird ringed in Spain that was later trapped by me at her nest with two chicks on a mountainside near Blaenavon, Wales!

It's common for resident stonechats to raise two families each breeding season and often three are managed. Their nest is built on or near the ground and very well hidden within the likes of heather, bracken, crowberry and bilberry. The eggs are similar in colour to the whinchat's but greener and more clearly marked with a rusty brown fleck. Five or six eggs is the normal clutch size and although brood sizes at ringing time can vary from two to six chicks, the average would be around five. The female may start building her nest as early as March and I have seen stonechat young from a third brood still in the nest in September. In the study area, the whinchat probably outnumbered the stonechat by roughly four to one breeding pairs. Today, 2024, these figures will be reversed within the study area in favour of the highly successful stonechat.

The Linnet (*acanthis cannabina*). The linnet is a busy little bird, forever active and always appearing to live life to the full. Slightly smaller than the house sparrow, this finch of the hillside likes nothing better than open areas of gorse, even at lower altitudes, such as our coastal districts. On the moorland edge, however, the linnet has done rather well for itself by nesting in tall lank heather bushes that are readily available. Despite them liking the heather, where rare stands or individual bushes of gorse are present, it's a good idea to search for the linnet's nest there too. It is another bird of the hillside that, although thought of as a resident species, can undertake local migrations of several kilometres and one suspects even longer movements are more than achievable. They arrive in pairs and small groups at the end of March and early April, just like other species on the hill. They then proceed to nest in loose colonies of several pairs or more, depending on the concentration of birds and the availability of suitable nest sites. The nest is a neat construction of grasses, and the cup is cosily lined with horsehair and sheep wool with the occasional feather. The female lays, in my experience, a clutch of four or five eggs, which are of a very pale blueish white in colour and streaked purple-brown. Two broods are common. I have witnessed a cuckoo egg in a linnet nest, but only once and, on this occasion, the whole nest was deserted, either intentionally or otherwise. Post-breeding season parties in the study area can grow to forty or fifty birds or more, as the young and parent birds roam the district in search of food together. They are extremely gregarious and are seemingly of a tolerant and gentle nature. Linnets, like other hill species, leave their breeding grounds in September-October in their quest to avoid the worst of the weather. They undoubtedly congregate with other finch flocks in lowland areas until winter is through.

Meadow Pipit (*anthus pratensis*). At first glance, the meadow pipit seems a nondescript little species, with its mainly brown-streaked plumage. But in the hand or at close quarters through the binoculars, it can be rather striking. This gentle and often overlooked bird is also of a rather interesting character. Like so many of the species that inhabit the moor in the spring and summer months, the meadow pipit leaves in droves in the autumn and is absent in all but the mildest of winters. Vast incoming movements can be witnessed over the valleys of the Welsh uplands during the months of March as the pipit makes its way to a higher altitude to breed in our hills. It builds a neat little nest on the ground, well hidden within a grass tussock, under a heather bush or other suitable ground cover. In the study area, four or five eggs are normal for a first clutch and three to four for a second. The eggs, though variable, are generally brown-grey in colouration and heavily streaked with darker brown, particularly on the larger end. The meadow pipit is also the prime choice as 'host' for the cuckoo in the hills and, every summer, recently fledged young cuckoos can be seen being fed by the attentive and unassuming parent pipits. This is interesting behaviour because earlier on during the season, the meadow pipit obviously recognises the cuckoo as a threat and an intruder and can be seen chasing and mobbing the 'parasite'. Yet here it is, having incubated the larger bird's egg, and brought up the giant demanding hatchling as its own, demonstrating the strongest of parental-youngster bonding you will ever witness.

The meadow pipit is also prone to bullying from the other species that share its habitat and is often chased relentlessly by others as it tries to return to the nest site. Many are also taken by birds of prey as they are by far the most numerous species on the open mountainside.

The Tree Pipit (*anthus trivialis*). A very close relative of the meadow pipit, the tree pipit is a typical migrant species arriving in this country in April and departing in August-September. In the study area, their emergence on the hillside is likened to their departure in that it goes largely unnoticed. For the tree pipit does not arrive in great numbers or large flocks like its aforementioned cousin but seems to be detected for the first time each spring by an explosion of individuals' song and its wonderful aerial display which accompanies a distinguished vocal delivery. The nest can be notoriously difficult to locate, with the adults being amongst the most vigilant of birds. Like that of the meadow pipit, it is a simple affair but as in both cases, is a neat and very well constructed article of dry grasses lined with hair and again well-hidden at ground level. Four to six eggs are laid in a typical clutch and there is sometimes a second or replacement nest. Compared to the more common meadow pipit, this species is only slightly different in appearance, especially at a distance and to the inexperienced observer, it can be a test telling them apart. However, the tree pipit seems to be overall a neater-looking bird, generally a more golden-brown in the right light with contrasting paler edges to the wing feathers and beautifully streaked with dark brown on the breast and back areas. Still, perhaps it is easier to separate both these species by their song and calls. Also, the tree pipit prefers the presence of scattered trees within its territory from which the male bird can sing and display. Such territories are often along the edge of a woodland or copse that connects to the hillside. This is why you don't generally see tree pipits on the open moorland tops like you will the meadow pipit.

Whinchat Ridge

The Skylark (*Alauda arvensis*). Like the numerous meadow pipit, the larger skylark prefers to vacate its hillside haunts in search of milder climes and a food supply that will see it through the lean winter months. But on milder days very early in March, the glorious and familiar song of the lark can be heard proclaiming the arrival of spring. These masters of creating joy and inspiring poetry can then be seen rising from the ground on quivering wings to a height of many metres until they are but a 'pinprick' to the naked eye, or indeed disappear from the view of the observer altogether. In the study area, the bulk of the skylark population tends to inhabit the higher ground further up the hill where there are plenty of grass tussocks and heather. They prefer this type of habitat and will build their nests on the ground there. The nests themselves are made of fine grasses and are often well hidden but by no means always so. Of the nests I have found, three-four eggs are the normal clutch size and two broods are common.

A word must be said about the young birds. While still in the nest and especially after fledging, juvenile skylarks are a joy to behold. Extremely well camouflaged, they lie motionless and are practically 'invisible' on grassy ground. They are so docile and gentle when handled and possess a most comical clown-like appearance, with immensely long fluffy down feathers that protrude from around the head and the rest of the upper body. It is thought, like so many other species these days, that skylarks are diminishing in numbers. Although in the study area they seem to be holding their own, we must be on our guard as I believe the greatest threat to the birds of the mountainside is habitat loss and the changing wet summer weather patterns. This makes the skylark and others vulnerable. The plight of the skylark on arable farmland is a different matter.

Steve J Smith

Female Whinchat Feeding Fledged Young Skylark

On 16th June, I was to witness something I had never seen before, at least not where the whinchat was concerned. While on a routine nest-finding exercise, and in familiar territory, I found myself scanning an area of suitable habitat with my field glasses, when I came across the pale form of a female whinchat standing out against the background of dark heather. She was gathering food and because I hadn't found a nest at this site this season, I became excited at the prospect of another whinchat brood to ring.

As I approached the area more closely and neared the spot where I had seen her repeatedly drop down with food, she began to call loudly at my presence. I then did what I always do at a time such as this, and retreated to a distance and hid, so that I could observed the hen whinchat as she came back to the suspected nest. This she did on several occasions. I then moved towards the site once again, confident that I was to find the nest there. I could not locate a nest, but while I was looking, I was startled by a young skylark as it took flight from under my feet. I continued my search to no avail. I tried and tried again, but after watching for some time, I became aware that the female chat was now taking food to another spot some short distance away from the original one. I was becoming frustrated and thought at first that she must have fledged young of her own and that they were on the move. So, still not totally convinced and with a sixth sense that comes with experience, I hid again and again to try and make sense of the situation. With all the activity at this time of year, with the young of several species all begging for food, making their first flights and calling to maintain contact, it took quite a bit of concentrated observing to come to the final and surprising conclusion.

Suddenly it became apparent that every time the female whinchat went to the ground amongst the deep vegetation with food, a young fledgeling skylark would appear in the same place. I then realised what was going on. The whinchat was indeed feeding the skylark. I have only seen this on one other occasion when a female blackbird was observed feeding young dunnocks still in the nest. The blackbird had lost the contents of her own nest, probably due to predation, and her motherly instinct and the urge to feed was so strong she had fostered the young dunnocks.

So, had the whinchat lost her own chicks and found the urge to mother the skylark too powerful to dismiss?

The Wheatear (*Oenanthe oenanthe*). This summer migrant spends winter in tropical Africa and is one of the first species to arrive back in the mountains after its long return journey to its nesting grounds. A striking little bird, not much bigger than a whinchat, the wheatear is always alert and very active. You can't mistake the plumage of either sex with the startling white rump and the strong contrasting black of the wings against a pale body the obvious give away. It is a bird which prefers open well-grazed areas where there are plenty of boulders or dry-stone walls to nest in or under. A construction of grass, lined with hair and feathers, contains an average of six uniform pale blue eggs. Bird numbers fluctuate annually and they have disappeared from some districts within the study area altogether. The male has a startling display flight, not unlike the whinchat, where it can be seen throwing itself up into the sky off an elevated perch, gaining a little height and flashing its white plumage while all the while singing loud and proud. It is a hardy species. I have seen the first wheatears of spring hopping around in small upland fields in search of food while the snow is on the ground or there is a thick fog and a strong wind. They are with us from the first week in March in some years and stay with us well into October when many other migrants have upped and left already. I have recorded the odd bird in November passing through.

The Reed Bunting (*Emberiza schoeniclus*) Most bird watchers will be used to seeing the reed bunting amongst deeply reeded areas around our inland waters or coastal fringes. This is a species that, in my experience, has adapted to living on dry hillside habitats in relatively recent years. It still seems more numerous on a mixed wet/dry heath though and seems to thrive in this habitat within the study area. The male bird has a black head and throat not unlike a male stonechat, with a deep chestnut-brown, heavily streaked back and white outer tail feathers. The female lacks the black head and neither possesses the red breast of the stonechat. Nesting from late April to July, and sometimes going into August, the nest is built very near to ground level and of local materials. In the case of the study area, this is usually dead stems of soft rushes that are very common, lined with finer grasses and horsehair. In recent years, I have discovered nests built in drier terrain, such as vast areas of bracken. Four to five eggs are laid, which are ground-colour lavender with a brownish tinge, or even ash grey boldly scribbled with brownish-black and grey. I have watched with interest as both sexes gather food for their young and then return to the nest or fledgling which may be nearly a kilometre away! A long, low and straight flight directly back is taken, and they are oblivious to all around them as they focus on the job of rearing the brood.

Yellow Hammer (*Emberiza citrinella*) To see a male yellow hammer is an amazing thing. The bright yellow head and breast of the bird is a glorious sight. It also has a back of rustic-chestnut brown heavily streaked with dark brown. Overall, a dapper little bird. We have 'lost' almost all our yellow buntings over the past 25 years or so for no obvious reason. A few pairs now nest on the Blorenge Mountain in part of the study area and the wonderful song of the male bird described as 'a little bit of bread and no cheese' conjures up images of mid-summer with sunny days and blue sky. Apart from the boldness of the male song, the yellow hammer is a shy bird, and all goes quiet when they are feeding young at the nest. They too are a species of farmland but are equally at home in the hillside habitat, especially where bracken is abundant. They can raise two or three broods if conditions are right and the weather favourable, going on until August. Four or five purplish-white eggs are laid, and these are characteristically streaked and scribbled with dark brown markings. Grasses and roots form the main structure of the nest, which is a rather deep cup, lined with hair and other fibres and very well hidden, low to the ground in the undergrowth.

Confrontation With a Cuckoo

At 7 o'clock in the evening on 17th June, I sat in deep heather and bilberry on the upper banks of southern Mynydd y Garn Fawr. It was a fine end to the day, and I had panoramic views of the gently sloping moorland fringe below me. I became aware that there was much activity from the local bird population. Suddenly I noticed a pair of whinchats, several hundred metres away, with their tiny pale bodies standing out clearly against the background of deep uniform dark heather. At first, I thought it obvious that the whinchat pair were showing aggression toward the neighbouring meadow pipits. As I went on to witness the repeated dives by the chats into the vegetation, all I could see was a flurry of wings resulting in a blur of activity through my binoculars. I still thought that this was a chat versus pipit confrontation and smiled at how stubborn the birds were. However, it soon became clear that both species had, in fact, joined forces in an attempt to see off a predator or threat of some kind. I left my vantage point in order to get closer to the scene of the action before the unknown cause of all the commotion had a chance to leave the area, leaving me none the wiser. As I approached the site, the whinchat pair retreated to approximately fifty metres, while two out of the three meadow pipits that were present reluctantly took flight as I stepped silently and slowly toward my destination. When the third pipit noisily reluctantly flew off, the cause of the anxiety among these small songbirds became apparent. On hawk-like wings, a cuckoo raised clumsily out of the dark, lank heather and reached for the sky, not a young reddish-brown bird being attended to by the gentle pipits, but a true-blue adult female bent on predation or persecution. Lazily the pirate flew away and immediately became the cause of even more concern to the local songbird population as it made its way low over many other occupied breeding territories.

There then followed a period of calm in the area, which lasted about two minutes, before suddenly the cuckoo came into my field of view as I watched the courting whinchat pair. The cuckoo seemed determined to gain access to the very same site. I had concluded that there was a pipit nest hidden there and the large parasitic migrant wanted to lay an egg in it at all costs! As it came closer, the cuckoo was mobbed all the way by hovering pipits. It was now that the male whinchat left its heather perch and flew in a determined fashion and at speed, straight towards the cuckoo and came within inches of the larger bird. This brave deed was accompanied by a vocal exclamation from the little protector in the form of a loud 'chat' uttered during its arrow-like flight into danger. The female whinchat was distantly involved all the while. Eventually the cuckoo gave up on this site, for now at least, and disappeared from view once more and all seemed calm on this part of the hill again.

Before very long, I observed a large female peregrine falcon as it flew southward over the upper ridge of the moorland. Now I became fearful for the lone cuckoo. Could the predator become the prey? Within minutes the falcon retraced her flight path and was northward bound once more, leaving the cuckoo alone for today and the chats and the pipits got on with their all-important courtship and breeding activities.

The Dartford Warbler

Sometimes, when routine field work is being carried out, something extra remarkable happens. This is the brief story of how I discovered the first breeding pair of Dartford warblers to nest in Wales. Below is the article that I wrote for the Gwent Bird Report way back in 1998:

Dartford Warbler Confirmed Breeding in Wales

Those members of the RSPB amongst us will have probably noticed in the Welsh supplement (*Y Barcud*) to their quarterly magazine *Birds*, that the Dartford warbler bred for the first time in Wales in 1998. This is a remarkable record given that they are normally restricted to the heathlands of southern England.

I can now reveal, albeit anonymously, that this successful breeding of one of Britain's rarest breeding birds was in fact in Gwent.

Since I first spotted the birds and confirmed their breeding success, I have become more than a little obsessed by this rare resident warbler. Not simply because of its rarity, but also because of their interesting nesting habits. I have also become rather protective of them, due mainly to their vulnerability and the possible threat to the habitat on which they depend. I am therefore keeping my fingers crossed for this pair's future success at this secret site.

Summarised below are some of the key dates and notes relating to my extraordinary find which involves a solitary pair making three attempts to breed between April and August 1998. Two of these attempts were successful, but the other sadly succumbed to a predator when the chicks were around nine days old.

25th May First sighting after unfamiliar alarm calls had gained my attention. Pair seen carrying food for young which were hidden somewhere in the heather. Both birds were very shy and skulking. Continuous alarm call. Unbelievable!

27th May Did not locate the actual nest but found recently fledged young birds, all laid neatly tight together in a bed of moss under a heather bush.

1st June Saw the family unit 150 metres away from nest site. Good views of male bird seen feeding fledglings on top of vegetation.

7th June Family group now about 300 metres from nest site, all hidden deep within bracken patch higher up the hill. Continuous contact and alarm calls heard.

21st June Male bird observed near original nesting site. Alarm call heard, female not seen. A second breeding attempt?

29th June Nest two discovered with four young about three days old in the vicinity of the original site. Noticed that after a parent bird took food to the nest, it would brood the chicks until its mate returned, swapping roles continuously.

5th July All four young are OK. Lovely, dark and alert, looking like 'fine porcelain' and looking up at me bright-eyed.

8th July Doom and gloom! The nest was found empty - unknown predator. No sign of an adult bird despite an intensive search of the area. Very disappointing.

15th July An accidental meeting with the male Dartford warbler some 300 metres from the last nest site. Full song and alarm call heard. Again, no female seen, fuelling my suspicion of a possible third clutch of eggs?

1st Aug   I began to imagine the possibility of a third brood. Female seen and alarm calls heard near to where the male sang on 15th July.

2nd Aug   Amazingly I found a third nest with three young in it, about three days old. Noted that food for the birds is now plentiful after a cold and wet June/July. I hid at a distance and marvelled at the antics of the Dartford pair.

10th Aug   The three young fledged on my arrival at the nest. I noticed one infertile egg still in the nest cup. More than able to cope, the young birds moved off toward the calling female. Success!

24th Aug   Iolo Williams, (then RSPB), came to see the site with regard to its future protection and was rewarded with brilliant views of the female Dartford feeding her young with bright green caterpillars.

1st Sept   Family group in full view today. Contact call heard as they moved out of some bracken and into some heather. Still only fifty metres from third nesting site.

October   No sightings despite regular searching.

9th Nov   After a day's birdwatching, I called in on the Dartford site, but did not record the birds. I decided to make another 'cold' search for the elusive first nest, which I had not found previously. This proved successful. To my delight I located it just three feet away from where I had seen the first brood way back in May.

16th Nov   Typical alarm call heard. A bird, probably the male, was seen about 200 metres above and to the south of the last known nest site.

9th Dec   The last record of the year. Alarm call heard, loud and clear during foggy conditions as the birds moved invisibly through the tall heather. I realised how much I relied on the birds calling to aid me in my detection. The warblers' plumage colouration and shy habits make them impossible to locate otherwise.

During that breeding season, and since then, I have thought long and hard about the Dartford warblers' future at this site. After all, so many breeding attempts by rare and scarce species are often 'one-offs' and simply a date in the record books, just as a sighting of a rare individual bird may be.

After much searching, I finally saw one of the Dartford warblers again on 15th March 1999. This bird, a silent male, was in the company of a pair of stonechats. I had long and clear views of the bird and was genuinely excited for the coming spring. However, there was a heavy fall of snow in April that spring. I never came across the Dartford warbler again until a single bird was observed in the company of a wren, both living in the heather during November 2000.

Obviously, I was convinced that another breeding attempt may take place the following spring. This was not to be, however. I had to wait another five years for the privilege of seeing another Dartford nest. In 2005, a single pair raised two broods and the following summer, there were up to three pairs, and it was that year I ringed my first young Dartford warblers. By now, the news was that the tiny, vulnerable little warbler was expanding its range in Britain, due largely to milder winters. They had reached the Midlands and were establishing themselves in other parts of Wales. Sadly however, they have not nested in my study area since 2005. But I'll not give up hope of seeing them again, and who knows what the future holds?

Predation, Threats and Mortality

Like so many bird species of the British countryside, the whinchat is under great pressure, with population trends indicating a sharp and increasingly worrying decrease in overall numbers. Migrant species travelling thousands of kilometres each year to arrive at our shores are of particular concern, with some of the common and numerous species of my youth plummeting to all-time lows and there being no single reason, easy remedy or short-term solution to the problem. I would suggest that a world without bird song is a world not worth living in.

Threats to the whinchat and much of the native wildlife come in many different guises. Here I am only touching on some of the natural and avoidable problems that can affect the relatively short lifespan of the small and well-travelled songster which is the whinchat.

Migration[8] is a mammoth achievement and the perils that the trans-Saharan migrant faces are extremely difficult to monitor. The ever-present threat of being attacked by birds of prey and adverse weather conditions are just a couple of things to contend with. Along with this, some European countries still murder our migrant songbirds and others indiscriminately, for both sport and food. Cruel practices on a large scale still go on despite an international outcry and sterling work by conservation bodies in many of those countries some of us still decide to holiday in.

---

[8] July 2024. Update. Due to reasons yet not fully understood, the numbers of whinchat and of other migratory birds have decreased greatly and are now a cause of concern.

Whinchat Ridge

After a migration which includes parts of the Sahara Desert, parts of Spain and Portugal, mountain ranges and a sea crossing, the whinchat arrives home from their wintering quarters in Africa. When I refer to 'home', I mean Britain and more intimately to me, this means the hills of Wales. For this is where 'my' birds choose to nest and bring up a family, if possible.

While in their breeding grounds, the threats are still ever-present, if not more so, for nesting time is an even more anxious period in the life cycle of the ground-nesting whinchat. The adult whinchat is cautious and speedy and experienced in staying safe. But they can be more vulnerable, especially at nesting time, when they are preoccupied with breeding duties. Avian predators are forever on the lookout for opportunities to snatch an adult bird from its territory on the open hillside or the inexperienced fledgling on its first forays into the big wide world. While carrion crows will spoil a nest, taking chicks and young birds of all ages, other avian threats come from raven, buzzard, sparrowhawk, hobby and several others. On the ground, adders will take chicks and eggs, while mammalian hunters such as stoat, weasel and fox are opportunists, always on the lookout for a satisfying meal.

One proven enemy is the sparrowhawk. You can witness this fact in the chapter linking the predatory sparrowhawk to breeding whinchats when we found several rings belonging to local whinchats at the nest sites of the hawks in forestry plantations.

Nesting whinchats have several survival actions which they use when there are chicks in the nest. If a nest containing young birds that are around eight days old or more is disturbed, then the whinchat's offspring can leave the nest prematurely. Individuals leaving on foot in many different directions therefore confuse a would-be predator or sometimes an unfortunate ornithologist! Also, when the young leave the nest after a full term in their 'nursery', they don't perch prominently for a week or so after vacating but spend the early days deep in the cover of the dense vegetation.

Of course, there's safety in numbers too, with neighbouring birds calling their alarm and distress call to warn others in the vicinity of their own territory.

Other threats and problems faced by the whinchat are numerous. It has long been suggested that the problems they face are complex and may even continue in their wintering quarters abroad. At 'home' on the breeding grounds, however, while the whinchat's habitat has remained relatively unaffected by change, in recent years at least, the number of birds returning to nest each year fluctuates. At the time of writing, the population within the study area is struggling, in my opinion due to climate change. The weather is key to many a failed or successful breeding season. Summers on the hills and elsewhere have become unpredictable, with a cold and wet summertime more common than we would like. This pattern of severe weather conditions is yet another nail in the coffin of a struggling ground-nesting songbird.

Little did I know how bad and steep this decline would continue to be. Summers have been cold or wet or sometimes both. Some mid summer's mornings I was wearing a jacket, gloves and a woollen hat. Although bright and dry most of the summer, there was a cold wind almost daily. It was obvious too that broods were smaller; mortality was up, and food availability was limited due to the temperatures.

During some seasons, when the weather in June or July has been wet or cold or both, it's not unusual for the whinchat to suffer greatly from high mortality rates at the nest, with chicks occasionally dying in large numbers. I have also found female birds dead on the nest twice over the years, though they had obviously died a natural death.

Apart from the weather, there are many other types of threats and obstacles for all ground-nesting birds that live on the open hillside and moorland edges. I have often recorded a fox manoeuvring its way through the tall bracken within the territory of breeding birds. Each time, it was a cause for concern for the birds and they showed their anxiety with loud alarms until the predator had ambled off out of sight. I know that the fox breeds in the study area, but I suspect that the damage done to the whinchat population by this mammal is rather minimal. It is my theory that if a fox has been at a whinchat nest, then the result is a total annihilation of the nest cup, eggs and young. Witnessing any such predation is very rare and the first the human recorder will know about it is when he or she visits the nest to collect further data.

Other mammals are present in the hillside habitat. The stoat and the weasel are renowned as ferocious hunters and are perfectly adapted to hunting at ground level where many songbirds on the moorland edge have their nests.

Another potential threat to the whinchat nest is the adder. I have half a dozen or so sightings of an adder each summer. These are mainly accidental occurrences as I go about my business of nest recording, but I am aware that they are breeding as they are constantly present. I have a record of an adder found in a whinchat nest after it had devoured some of the chicks. *(see special notes).* I am convinced that the adder is probably responsible for many more losses at nest sites.

There are several avian predators that are a constant threat to the nest contents and the life of the adult whinchats also. Of these, the crow family are well represented, with carrion crow, magpie and 'King of the hill', the raven, always on the lookout for a free meal, whether it be a clutch of eggs or a brood of defenceless chicks or even an inexperienced, immature bird in its early days of flight.

The biggest threat to the adult population comes from the true birds of prey. Species like the sparrowhawk are a constant problem, especially when the hawk is nesting in a nearby forestry plantation, for example. We have proved that sparrowhawks take whinchats and other songsters off the hill, through a study that found rings of birds at the predators' nests. *(see Whinchat/Sparrowhawk Study).*

The peregrine falcon, which nests in local quarries, is also a constant threat despite its preference for larger prey at times. Others like the kestrel and hobby are, in my opinion, more likely to make a target of other prey, though at fledging time these species will attack the immature birds, given the chance. Buzzards and K-kites are not a real problem, relatively speaking, and the merlin is very rare in the study area at nesting time.

Our local birds have many other threats and predators. Our garden birds are plagued by natural predators such as the much-hated species, the magpie. The haters of such natural predators are the same people who adore the grey squirrel and above all, the worst of the worst, some domestic cats. The domestic cat has a lot to answer for, in my opinion. Some years ago, I had a ringing recovery of a whinchat killed by a cat, which is probably extremely rare, given the whinchat's choice of habitat.

Human disturbance, either intentional or born out of ignorance, is on the increase and during the Covid pandemic our local mountains and beauty spots took a hammering. Also, small hamlets and villages that lie at the foot of the mountains and valleys below are growing at a rate that scares me, as they become townships with little thought for the infrastructure that's required to support such growth. The growing human population will ultimately drive into the countryside and wilder places on their doorstep. More pressure, more cars, more people, more litter and anti-social behaviour. I understand that most people are considerate and willing to treat the countryside with respect but with growing footfall comes a higher percentage of idiotic behaviour.

A few gripes and concerns and with a risk of controversy

Some of the other culprits, and wholeheartedly worth a moan at, include fly-tippers, arsonists, twitchers, falconers, gun dog trainers, drone pilots, off-road vehicles and land managers bent on shooting birds. Outside the nesting season, of course, some of these activities are more acceptable than others.

As always, not all the individuals involved in these pastimes are so inconsiderate and are at least willing to listen to my point of view.

Here are a few observations I've made over the years with some examples.

> Gun dog trainers who decide that teaching their dogs how to retrieve etc over heather moorland during the peak of the bird breeding season is acceptable. This is particularly problematic when they gather in one place for hours on end.

> Drone pilots who fly low over nesting terrain when birds are feeding their chicks at the nest and decide it's a good idea to pursue larger birds in flight are totally out of order. Drones flown irresponsibly can also be seen as an avian predator by small birds.

> While falconers do good work in some ways, I have had words with one or two about the seasonal effects of flying for long periods of time over the nesting habitat of our wild birds.

> Arson, in many people's opinion, is one of the most devastating crimes committed against wildlife and warrants punishment, especially during the months of April through to August when, as well as affecting helpless ground nesting birds, fire can devastate populations of reptiles and mammals too. The anxiety caused to the caring and understanding person also warrants a mention.

> Twitchers. Who would have thought I'd have any objection to fellow twitchers. First, I am not a twitcher, I am an ornithologist with a genuine love of birds. Now, I know many twitchers will have just as much compassion as I do. But one experience of a gathering of twitchers leaves me with a bad taste in my mouth. It was a few years ago when a rare bird turned up on Blorenge mountain and as far as I was concerned it couldn't have happened at a

worse time. I made some friends that summer, but I met the worst type of birder also, one without any interest in the local bird population which I was studying at the very time of the twitching intrusion. The breeding season was in full swing and hundreds of people turned up from all over the country, causing an unprecedented disturbance. It's an experience I'd rather forget.

➤ When discussing land management, I refer to the management for grouse shooting and possibly farming methods. I know that cattle are one of the best natural conservation grazing tools; however, in recent years I have proven that a concentrated grazing pattern of heavy animals can have a detrimental effect. In my opinion they should not graze the hill during the breeding season of ground nesting birds. They trample, lay and feed in sensitive areas and shouldn't be there twenty-four seven all year round. The lighter sheep don't seem to have any effect on such issues.

➤ Another issue on the moor is the natural regeneration of trees. I love trees and we should plant more. The problem is if we don't remove young trees from the heathland it ceases to be heathland. We will lose species that can't adapt to woodland and are already struggling, with many of them decreasing in numbers and in danger of vanishing. They need all the help they can get. The red tape involved in getting work done on the hill is immense and always a stumbling block with various countryside organisations, graziers and conservationists all vying to protect their own interests. Things can move slowly, or not at all. It could be our downfall in protecting our landscape for wildlife.

Whinchat Ridge

As I have said about not disturbing the ground-nesting bird life, I have had bad experiences with all the above and have had polite words with many individuals, but in the end, ignorance is everywhere.

Steve J Smith

Predation at the Nest by an Adder

I believe that predation by adders is more common than has been recorded. They are perfectly adapted to seek out and find the eggs and young of small ground-nesting species such as whinchats. But although we know that the adder population is probably thriving within the study area, actual proof in the form of eyewitness accounts of adder predation is very rare. On 11th June, I routinely visited a nest on the Blorenge Mountain to ring the chicks in a whinchat nest that I had found on a previous field trip. On my arrival at the nest, I became aware that at least one of the young birds was lying dead on the ground a little distance away from the actual nest site within a bilberry bush. This is not an uncommon sight to me, but I immediately knew that something did not seem quite right. It was just then that an adder caught my eye near the deceased chick. The female viper was also motionless; however, she became more alert when I purposely stamped the ground with my walking stick. I wanted to check the actual nest, but I didn't want any nasty surprises from the snake. I was OK with her presence, so long as I knew her whereabouts. The adder then proceeded to make its way back into the nest where I was convinced she had already been. I had clear views of it as it lay coiled up and she was once again quite content to keep very still. After a wee period of contemplation, I decided to leave the nest site to undergo the short journey back to my vehicle where my camera lay idle. After my swift and energetic return to the nest, I discovered that the adder had taken the opportunity during my absence, to silently slip away. Below is the nest record data which includes the actual event.

NEST No. 35-96 near Paddock wall, Carn-y-Gorfydd, the Blorenge Mountain.

Nest at ground level and within a bilberry bush.

1st July: Both parents feeding 4+ chicks. Hatching/ eggs. Female occasional brooding.

8th July: Male and female feeding at the nest. Both trapped for ringing.

Female= K487797. Male=K487798. Both 'new birds'.

11th July: Returned to check brood. Discovered adder at nest. One dead chick outside nest. When disturbed, snake hid in nest.

Ringing

As most of you will know, the ringing of wild birds in Britain is a strictly monitored operation, one in which the participant must undergo a full and comprehensive training programme. Ringing permits are renewed annually and every ringer must abide by the rules and regulations set down by the British Trust for Ornithology and the law of the land. Such rigorous rules need to be set down because, without strict monitoring and training, unnecessary suffering could be caused - for example, desertion of the nest by the adult birds, ill-fitting rings, injury to the bird etc. The bird always comes first. The situation is always assessed and the ringer must use good judgement when deciding whether or not to ring, taking into consideration adverse weather conditions and several other factors, such as the individual bird's character etc. If the adult bird is struggling to feed itself or its offspring, leave well alone. Personally, I feel privileged to be able to handle wild birds for the purpose of science and ultimately a greater understanding of birds leading to their conservation.

For many years I have concentrated my efforts largely on the whinchat and contribute a massive amount to the annual tally of whinchats ringed in Britain. I have trapped and processed hundreds of adult whinchats and ring an average of 200-300 chicks every summer. The personal excitement of this is marred only by the stress caused to the bird at the time of handling, although this is always kept to a minimum by a well-trained and sympathetic ringer. I feel it's for the greater good that I carry out this work and after all these years of ringing, I can honestly say no bird has suffered physically in my hands or deserted the nest because of my actions.

Young whinchats are in the nest for up to fourteen days and are ideally ringed at around one week old. However, they can successfully be handled between five and ten days old, but care must be taken with the older brood, as juvenile chats can leave the nest at any stage after nine days old if disturbed by a predator or a ringer. This is a survival strategy which, in periods of warm weather with well-fed, well-grown chicks, enables the young birds to scatter, therefore ensuring some success.

When someone finds and reports a ringed bird, it's called a recovery. A bird can be caught alive and reported by another ringer anywhere in the world, or it may be found dead somewhere. All information is valuable, though recoveries of small migrant songbirds like the elusive whinchat are rare.

During the late 90s, the British Trust for Ornithology introduced the 'Re-trapping Adults for Survival' project or RAS. The aims of this intense and concentrated field work were to trap or re-trap as many as possible of the adult population of a chosen species in a defined study area over a period of several years, to assess the survival rates. At its peak, the study produced some important data. It was proven that whinchats are very site-loyal when up to 75% of adult birds were shown to return to their place of birth or at least to the location where they were originally ringed as an adult at the nest. When a study is so intensive, it is possible to 'get to know' individual birds and their life histories. This is the most rewarding part of working closely with your bird. Where it nested last year, the ID of its mate and the breeding details at the nest, who its parents are, how old the bird is, the 'mileage on its clock' etc. etc., all information gained through ringing and hard work in the field.

The Predation of Whinchats by Sparrowhawks

A study of Whinchat ringing recoveries at Sparrowhawk nests

Quite some years ago, I met fellow ornithologist Mark Lawrence in Crickhowell. He was a man whose interest in the whinchat was in its infancy back then, but to find another who had any interest for 'my' bird was remarkable. Since that day, our friendship has flourished, and we went on to share many hours in the field, nest-finding and sharing data between ourselves.

It was while discussing Mark's work of searching peregrine nest sites for the rings of birds the falcon had taken, that we decided to try and start a similar project by searching near the local sparrowhawk sites in the autumn. After all, as we often saw the hawk hunting on the hill which joins the forestry less than a kilometre away, then the predator was more than likely taking the odd whinchat as well as other species that nest there. Some of these birds would be ringed, simply because of the high number I put rings on.

The thought of finding the rings of 'my' birds initially filled me with excitement for scientific reasons and we went ahead with some preliminary work in a forest near Blaenavon. By now, I was half-hearted about the exercise, the excitement ultimately becoming sadness, as any retrievals would signify the deaths of the birds. But my scientific mind won out and we carried on.

The following year, we returned to the larch forest at Blaenavon with renewed hope and enthusiasm to kick start our study in earnest. It took us very little time in locating what turned out to be the previous season's nest site where we thought that the sparrowhawk had been successful. This we labelled site number one. During our initial searches under this nest, which was around 30 feet or so up in a larch tree, we became aware that there was a hawk family occupying the area directly below us. The female and several immature birds could be seen and, above all, heard as prey was being delivered high in the canopies of the surrounding woodland.

Back at site one, we decided to climb the nesting tree and the old nest of twigs was brought to the ground in order to investigate it at close quarters for clues. Amazingly, that evening, our first two tiny rings were found under the nest site and a neighbouring tree. A combination of skill with a metal detector and the keenness of a sharp eye had brought forth the results we had dreamt of. The individual ring numbers immediately rang a bell with me, and I knew that both were originally fitted to whinchats in my study area. I was overwhelmed with joy at first, but later some sadness crept in when the 'scientific cap' I was wearing had slipped and I thought of the plight of my beloved whinchats in the claws of such a formidable hunter. Yet I still craved for more information that only this sort of study could produce.

Several days later, we returned to site one and carried out one of the most thorough searches possible, spending hours scanning with the detector and manually sifting through the debris below the nest tree and others for clues. That day, the fate of another of my birds was uncovered when a third ring was found in the same location as the previous two.

Back at home, I flicked through the pages of my record books to establish the history of each whinchat whose life had been taken by the sparrowhawk to feed its own demanding youngsters. Despite the mixed emotions that I felt, I was amazed at the information and knowledge gained by our project as I studied the details of each of the lives of the 'lost' whinchats.

Much has been achieved since the start of our study at site one. It has become an extremely valuable part of my understanding of the full life story of the whinchat. Our finds and the details of further discoveries are summarised in the following table.

Table of ringing and finding information for rings found				
Species	**Ringing Date**	**Ringing Location**	**Finding Date**	**Other Info**
Whinchat	17.06.00	Garn Fawr	31.07.01	RAS Pullus
Whinchat	07.06.00	Blorenge	31.07.01	RAS Pullus
Whinchat[1]	10.06.98	Garn Clochdy	04.08.01	RAS Male
Whinchat	22.06.00	Blorenge	06.08.01	RAS Female
Whinchat	20.06.01	Garn Clochdy	10.08.01	RAS Pullus
Whinchat	21.06.95	Garn Clochdy	19.08.01	Pre-RAS
Whinchat	23.06.96	Garn Clochdy	19.08.01	Pre-RAS
Whinchat[2]	03.06.00	Blaen Onneu, Powys	21.08.01	RAS Female
Whinchat	02.07.01	Garn Clochdy	27.08.01	RAS Male
Pied Flycatcher[3]	09.05.00	Nr Rifton, Devon	21.08.01	RAS Female
Whinchat	14.06.99	Garn Clochdy,	08.09.01	RAS Pullus
Greenfinch	27.04.99	Lasgarn Wood,	08.09.01	Garden Pullus
Meadow Pipit[4]	15.07.90	Garn Clochdy	11.11.01	RAS Area
Whinchat	13.06.95	Garn Clochdy	18.11.01	Pre-RAS
Wheatear	04.06.93	Varteg	--.12.01	Nest Box Pullus

All locations are in Gwent, unless otherwise specified

1. RAS - Re-trap adult survival. A project set up by British Trust for Ornithology to determine the survival rates of birds in a given study area.
2. Pre-RAS - before the above project was under way.
3. Pull - (Plural Pulli). A young chick in the nest.
4. All called Pullus/Pulli whether in nest boxes or natural site.

Photography

I have never owned a nice camera until now. Most of my photographs are the result of pocket cameras and more recently, mobile phone images. Such images have been of the brood in the nest, or a lovely clutch of eggs, while the bird in the hand allows for quite decent close-ups. I must admit though, that the yearning for a decent camera has grown stronger as time goes on. Just something to catch the bird in its natural pose on a fence post, dry stone wall or the top of a heather bush perhaps. Then there's the part of me that thinks I'm more privileged than most top photographers, having held hundreds of wild birds, and particularly my whinchats, in my clumsy human hands. I have held them gently while peering into their knowing eyes. I have held the same bird on several different occasions after it had nested and journeyed back and forth, to and from Africa before our meeting again. So, you see, I've never felt the need until now to collect images while I had the real thing so close to me.

Wildlife photography and in particular, bird photography, has taken off massively over the last decade or two and it strikes me it has turned into a bit of a competition, like so much linked to birds these days. I have witnessed first-hand one element of modern photographers who care more about the result of their efforts than the wellbeing of the subject. But while it's the same in ringing and twitching, with ignorance and poor behaviour in a minority, there are some very passionate skilful 'birders' out there as well as some truly amazing photographers.

It is here that I'll again mention my friend of 30 years, Dave Lock. Dave is a great man behind the camera but also a generally good person with a genuine love of birds. We first came together when Dave fancied a go at capturing some whinchat activity on Mynydd Garn Clochdy near my home. Though he had to travel a wee bit, Dave wouldn't rush anything. He would arrive and I'd take him to a whinchat territory and a likely pair for him to work on. The rest was then down to him. He would unfurl his home-made hide, assess the landscape and watch the birds to gather information on the way this pair moved and their favoured perching positions etc. Dave would then lay his un-erected canvas hide on the ground so that the birds got used to it after we had left. On another visit, the hide would be raised to maybe half the full height and then, of course, on his return, he reaped the benefits by taking the most wonderful pictures of my birds in close-up.

Filming at the Nest

When it comes to video recording, the story is much the same: the use of amateur equipment and a reliance on field craft and an in-depth understanding of your subject. I have learnt so much about my bird by simply hiding a movie camera near the nest and it's always exciting watching the footage back and seeing what the results are. I've also learnt to take still images from the video film. Though the quality is not there, the results are above average, I feel.

At the turn of the millennium, I produced a home-made video about a season with the birds, focusing on the whinchat, of course, and even added some emotional music and self-interviews. I still have it today but, unfortunately, it's recorded onto VHS and so has lost some quality. I would still dearly love someone who knows what they're doing to follow me for a season and film me going about my time on the hill. I'd like to be behind the camera because I know exactly what I'd require but it's difficult being in two places at once. A musical score would be a must for me; I'm a great fan of suitable music with any filming.

I have found it both a privilege and most revealing to film whinchats at the nest. I have discovered that there is 'another language' used by parent birds when at the nest together; I have watched in close up the interaction between a protective hen bird and an intruding male wren and had rewarding views of the food items the adult whinchats have brought as offerings to their chicks. I have observed with concern while a lone female struggles to bring up her brood after her partner was taken by a predator. All these and more have enlightened my study and filled in some of the gaps of missing knowledge that I longed to understand. Here are some short notes regarding some of the happenings while filming at the nests of breeding whinchats.

Once the camera was set up and I vacated the site, the female whinchat came back to the nest and entered the site without pausing. A male then arrived at the nest where the female was sitting on four eggs, dropping down with no offering of food. The camera sound mic picked up a 'conversation' between the intimate pair. The female call was rather quiet and sounded like a bubbling submissive and gentle warble, almost continuous. The male answered with a type of subtle sub-song, again rather quiet. More calls were forthcoming before the male left the nest and the hen stayed to keep the eggs warm.

At another nest, the camera was left on the ground as normal and again I crept away to let things settle. A male never visited this nest in all the visits I made. The female worked hard to bring food to four hungry, week-old chicks and was extremely busy. Every now and then, a male wren could be heard singing in the background on early footage. After a while, the wren made an appearance very close to the nest and even looked inquisitively into the site once or twice at the gaping young whinchats. The female's reaction was quick and authoritative. She would chase the boisterous wren away time and again as he continued to take an interest in the whinchat's brood. Finally, she succeeded.

Television

I got rather used to being interviewed by the media during my time as a Countryside Ranger - national news for one thing or another, and the 50th anniversary DVD of the Brecon Beacons National Park. In my own time too, I've been interviewed on the radio and the TV news on a totally different subject...my rare breed sheep which I keep for conservation grazing.

One TV appearance has given me more recognition than any other. It makes me laugh that every time it's repeated, someone will have seen me and mention it at some stage. The programme is about the four seasons of the Brecon Beacons National Park, its places, people and especially its wildlife, and was introduced by our very own Iolo Williams. I first met Iolo when he worked for the RSPB and came to witness my discovery of the first nesting pair of Dartford warblers in Wales on our moorland edge[9]. This is briefly how I became involved in an episode while sharing details of my beloved whinchats and the work I do while studying them.

---

[9] There are some notes on this is a previous chapter.

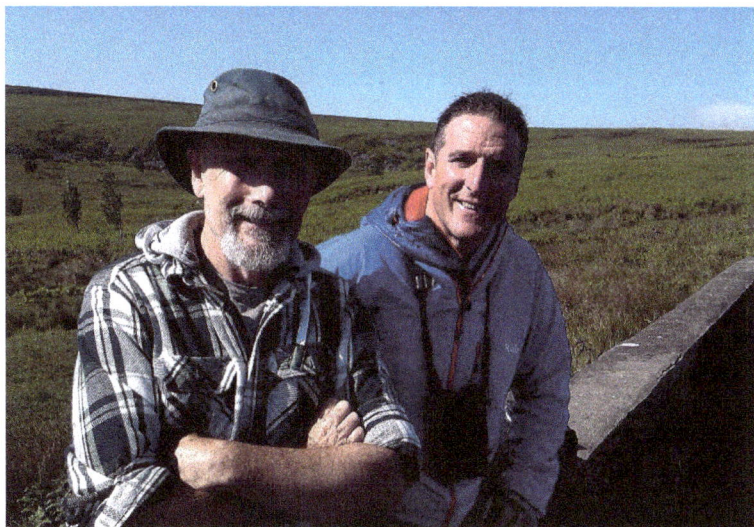

The Brecon Beacons with Iolo Williams

It was in early 2015, while carrying out some routine work as a Brecon Beacons National Park warden that I found myself in conversation with a young chap whose task it was to bring together ideas for a planned forthcoming TV programme about the people, wildlife, landscape and history of the Brecon Beacons and the 1344 square kilometres which the park covers. During our conversation, I mentioned my other 'job' as an unpaid fieldworker and a volunteer ornithologist and wild bird ringer with the British Trust for Ornithology and in particular, my life-long and intensive study of my beloved whinchat. Also key was that one of my main study areas is the Blorenge mountain ridge which lies in the southeast of the National Park and if needed, I would gladly contribute to any future filming. Nothing more was said until, out of the blue, came an email confirming that the production company would like to include me at work ringing on the mountainside as part of the summer edition of the four seasonal episodes to be aired in the not-too-distant future.

The day of the recording came. It was Midsummer's Day, and I had a few whinchat nests to choose to ring at and for the film crew to consider. On my early arrival at the meeting place, I pulled into the car park on the mountainside that affords spectacular views of the Usk Valley and Monmouthshire down below. My arrival was greeted by Iolo and three other crew members already taking hot tea and cake as a makeshift breakfast. The morning was so cold for mid-summer and all in attendance were wearing coats, hats and even gloves! I remember commenting that there were no flying insects on the very bright, dry, yet extremely cold morning.

It soon became obvious that the birds were struggling for food and the sympathetic crew and I agreed that, for the sake of the birds, there would be no time for several repeated takes during filming. There turned out to be no problem in achieving a professional and faultless sequence. Having met Iolo several times before and with a crew that knew their job well, I was made to feel at ease, and all went smoothly and to plan. I ringed a brood and chatted to Iolo near the nest and some footage of the Whinchat pair returning to the nest afterwards completed the recording.

Since the programme was aired originally, it has been repeated several times on various channels and every time, my small contribution is recognised by friends, family and acquaintances when we meet up or over the phone. A slice of fame for my Whinchats.

Then, almost ten years later (June 2024), practically the same film crew required my help regarding whinchats and their habitat once again. So we took to Mynydd Garn Clochdy and filmed a successful sequence for a future S4C TV documentary.

Foot and Mouth

Foot and mouth is a devastating disease that has done crippling damage to an already struggling agricultural industry. I have very strong views and opinions on this subject. However, this is not the time or the place to express my personal thoughts on the whole sorry affair. Common sense will tell you who suffered the most from this foot and mouth outbreak for month after month as, apart from the animals themselves and the farming community, tourism and its associated businesses suffered. I would say it affected the likes of me also. This claim may sound selfish to some, but I am sure I wasn't alone in feeling a loss of freedom as well as a terrible sadness for the plight of the animals above all. As a passionate animal lover and living in a rural community where I have several friends who are sheep farmers, I felt the strain immensely. Finally, I was blocked from walking my beloved hills as I obeyed all strict rules of quarantine and stayed off the vegetation on the moorland and especially farmland. I felt imprisoned and helpless, and the lack of opportunity to exercise my obsession with the moors and the birds that inhabit them was a cause of anguish within me.

Throughout the winter of 2000 and the spring of 2001, all I could think about, like so many other people, was how and when this terrible disease would be eradicated, and things return to relative normality. As April 2001 approached, my personal state of anxiety rose to an all-time high. I had recorded my first whinchat on the 26th of the month and knew that soon the nesting season would start. I could not imagine a summer without access to the moors and the whinchats.

Eventually my hopes were realised. Locally the footpaths to the hills were opened at the end of May, which in theory, was just in time for my study to continue. Whinchats lay their eggs in May and June, with the early broods hatching the first week of the latter. So, though I had not missed much, I would have to work a little harder to collect my season's data. In the end, the season would seem shorter and filled, for me, with unusually high levels of tension.

Later in the summer, while working on my last two whinchat nests on the Blorenge, the news came through that the dreaded foot and mouth had returned. This time, it was nearer to home, and we were in for another period of quarantine. It was the end of July and another breeding season with the chats but the beginning of another period of worry and concern.

By October, our local paths reopened once again and the word was that we had beaten foot and mouth, at least for now.

The Camping Trips

The tranquillity and beauty of spending the night on a hilltop and waking up there at sunrise is a wonderful thing.

During the early days of the study, I spent a few nights in the company of my younger brother doing just that. We had selected and specially prepared a site on a plateau surrounded by deep vegetation and with panoramic views of not only Garn Clochdy and the study area but of Mynydd Varteg Fawr and Coity mountains also.

On a summer's night while watching the sun go down and the daylight seeming to last forever, the soul is filled with peace and joy, and when the cuckoo calls until 10.30pm as the last of the sun's rays disappear westward, you feel at one with nature and the birds you love so dearly.

On one occasion, a whinchat sang near our tent. It was pitch dark and all else was silent, but I stirred to the heavenly sound of my bird sending out its territorial warning notes which carry a great distance as they cut through the calmness of the predawn on the wild moor. I have never witnessed this before from the whinchat, but I guess you must spend the night on location to appreciate things fully.

Barely as the light appeared, the increase in avian activity was notably marked. Of course, as observers and field workers, we were up early while the birds were at the peak of their daily activity, feeding young in and out of the nest, singing and calling as well as chasing one another in a frenzy of territorial aggression. Despite all this, the air was still, and the quiet hum of insects increased in volume and intensity as the coolness of early dawn gradually gave way to the increasing warmth of the rising sun and the dew evaporated in front of your very eyes.

In the evening, the activity peaked once more as the birds that were feeding chicks in the nest strove to fill the bellies of their ever-hungry and demanding offspring before nightfall.

While our primary objective was to locate and record the whinchat population, other species were prominent all around in their breeding activities. Apparent was the rise and fall of skylark song, the high-pitched peeping of busy meadow pipits, the continuous cuckoo calling, and the gregarious linnet in family groups or pairs in flight back to their nests in tall heather. The stonechat was prominent too while the buzzards were high on summer thermals and the ravens croaked and tumbled acrobatically in the cloudless blue sky.

Great days and good weather, but as we know, the climate of our Welsh uplands, even in summer, is unpredictable. But we were lucky that year and everlasting memories were forged.

Another summer has now ended...

The strong south-westerly blows the promise of a storm and signals its intention to release the freshness of autumn upon us. The sentinel-like Blorenge Mountain stands dominant over Abergavenny town lying neatly in the cup of the valley down below. The Sugar Loaf, a neighbour of the Blorenge, soaks in the rays of the weakening summer sun, while the Skirrid stands proud in its historic venue, the most rugged of Monmouthshire's famous trio. There's a ghostly silence, apart from the wind which hugs the grazing sheep as these hardy creatures contemplate another winter in their homelands. All around, wild birds of the hill are feeding up in a frenzy of activity for the migration facing so many of them. Nature's call cuts through the air of anticipation like the scythe-like swift through the twilight skies of midsummer. Grasses are showing a yellow complexion, while the bracken mirrors gold and shades of rust brown, all fading like the memories of yet another summer in these fair Welsh hills. The rowan and hawthorn which line the Llanellen lane are laden and heavy with their bounty of ripening red berries, the favourite food of the forthcoming winter thrushes. For soon they will come, riding on the cold northerly winds in waves of thousands, collectively gathering at traditional sites to brighten our short winter days with their continuous chatter as they spread tales of intrigue from Northern lands.

Epilogue

Well, I have come full circle. Over 35 years of studying my beloved whinchat. Of course, I will never stop watching and finding a few nests every summer for as long as I am able, but the intensity of the study is over, and it is time to simply enjoy the bird in more mellow terms. I have seen them peak and thrive as a breeding species in the hills and valleys of Wales and I have recently witnessed their demise and fall into the ever-growing category of amber-listed species of British birds that were once regarded as common or numerous. Now the energy-sapping honeymoon period of my intensive study is over and age and other commitments are increasingly against me, along with the reduction in numbers of my subject, I have decided that I would enjoy every moment with my bird before it is too late, one way or another. I am sure they will still be breeding on my local hillside long after my day and I hope this delightful European songbird, along with many other species, can recover from its current situation and become common in numbers once more. It is not about man managing the land, at least not locally as the habitat has not changed over the years. I hope I'm wrong, but with the ever-growing human population and the interference and mismanagement of man causing unrelenting pressure on our countryside, the future looks bleak through my concerned eyes. There seems to be a growing trend of countryside activists and proactive conservationists who are, in my opinion, 'salt of the earth' but the activities of countryside so-called sports - shooting and hunting and cruelty to animals - and the ruining of habitats in the name of so-called progress are still prominent in our society. We must not give up, but money and corruption are strong enemies and I often have sleepless nights about such travesties that I have no control over.

But still I have the greatest of memories of my time spent with the whinchat. The individual birds I got to know through ringing. The heartbreak as well as the good times. The stress of the summer's inconsistent and sometimes downright awful weather. My wife will bear witness to the fact that I was hell to live with when things went against my bird in any way.

I remember the sun on my back and the rain down my neck as I practically lived with the birds all summer, lying deep in the bracken and heather, totally engrossed for hours on end in what I was doing. I marvelled at every nest found and still do to this day. Each hidden treasure is a little gem. I shared the whinchat's secrets and natural beauty. I am totally obsessed with them. I have the whinchat etched into my soul and my very being.

The Papers

A Study of Whinchats (*Saxicola Rubetra*) on the Moorland Edge

Summary

A study of breeding birds has been ongoing on sections of the Gwent moorland fringe since 1986. The main objective of the study is to obtain a greater understanding of whinchat breeding biology and its requirements. As many nests as possible are found every year while an average of 250 young whinchats are ringed each summer. An effort is made to trap, re-trap and control the adult breeding population within the study area and over the last three years (1999-2001) the average adult trap has been 95 birds. The re-trap rate has risen annually to 70% during 2001. Overall, both sexes were found to return to their birthplace in equal numbers. The choice of nest site has been well recorded from the start of the study, with particular attention to vegetation type and the direction in which the nest entrance faced. Results showed that the whinchats in the study area had a preference for bilberry for nest cover when available, and most often built their nest facing in a south by south/east direction.

Breeding summaries to determine each season's success are produced every year to assess egg laying productivity, average clutch and brood sizes and overall success. Breeding densities have also been calculated over many seasons.

Steve J Smith

Welsh Bird Report 2

These densities varied from site to site and were around 1 pair every three hectares at best, while the least populated sites had a density of 1 pair for every 7 hectares of suitable habitat. The breeding population of the study area has remained relatively stable since 1986. However, some local decline has been obvious, and the species seems to be receding from its southern outposts. While its relative, the stonechat (Saxicola torquata), has enjoyed unrivalled success in recent years, there is cause for concern regarding the whinchat's future. The study continues today with emphasis still on the RAS study (*Re-trap Adults for Survival*) project set up by the British Trust for Ornithology, and hopefully contributing to the survival of the species and its habitat.

Introduction

These days in Gwent, the whinchat as a breeding species is almost entirely restricted to the hill in the north and west of the county. The whinchat was chosen as a study species for several reasons. Above all, the *saxicola* species were under-studied and their link with the threatened moorland landscape made it a dual-purpose study. It was hoped to gain a greater understanding of the flora and fauna of the upland habitat with a view to contributing to any subsequent conservation requirements. In the *Gwent Atlas of Breeding Birds* (Tyler et al 1987), the county population was given as 450 breeding pairs. This figure, later contested when the population estimate was regarded as too high, was defended by Tyler et al (1995), and the author of this paper agrees that the original estimate was a little low rather than a little high.

During the late 1970s, some ringing of whinchat in small numbers was carried out by Playford et al, and since then, the only work carried out on whinchat of any significance in the county was along the 220m contour of the Henllys to Penyrheol ridge where it was estimated that 77 pairs nested.

(Boyland 1980). Unfortunately, some previous studies were brief, though a study that ran for four years on the Powys/Gwent border (M. Lawrence), proved valuable when comparisons could be made with the ongoing Gwent project. Interaction between the two projects has no doubt contributed to a greater understanding of the breeding biology and the needs of the whinchat in this region of Wales.

The Study Area

The study area is a relatively small section of Gwent moorland and bracken-covered ffridd[10] that is typical of other upland districts which dominate the north and west of the county. The site regarded as the study area has quite well-defined boundaries and consists of three different mountains interlinked. To the south, Mynydd Garn Clochdy with its gently rising slopes reaches a modest 420m. (SO2806 at the centre). Further north, Mynydd y Garn Fawr (SO2709) reaches 480m at its peak. Garn Fawr melts into the Blorenge (552m) at Carn-y-Gorfydd (SO2711). Not all mountainous or moorland habitat is suitable for breeding whinchats and experience has shown that the preferences of the species within the study area are obvious. (see results - choice of nesting sites).

The main vegetation species providing ground cover and ultimately nest sites are bracken (*Pteridium aquilinum*), bilberry (*Vaccinium myrtillus*), heather (*Calluna vulgaris*), Crowberry (*Empetrum nigrum*), cowberry (*Vaccinium vitis-idaea*), cross-leaved heath (*Erica tetralix*) and thereafter a variety of grasses, mosses and soft rushes which are typical of Welsh moors with a mixture of wet and dry habitats.

---

[10] A specific type of upland habitat in Wales, often described as the transition zone between enclosed farmland and open moorland or mountainside. It's a diverse area characterised by a mosaic of vegetation types, including heath, bracken, scrub and scattered trees, as well as rocky outcrops and wet flushes.

Welsh Report 3

While an in-depth study of the flora of the area is ongoing, some noteworthy species are bog asphodel, yellow iris, and the heath spotted orchid that inhabit the damper places. Tree specimens are both sporadic and localised, depending on the location. These trees mostly consist of saplings or ageing stunted individuals including rowan, lodgepole pine and hawthorn. On the Blorenge mountain for example, relatively small and scattered haws are reasonably frequent and relatively mature oaks occupy the gullies and climb the steep slopes to greet the whinchat's terrain there. At all sites, as the altitude increases, the lack of trees becomes more apparent. At all three locations, particularly Garn Clochdy, the moorland edge finally gives way to pastureland used by hill farmers to graze sheep or for hay making. These small hill farms are separated from the moor by stone walls, fences and on Garn Clochdy, lines of fairly mature beech trees, which are obviously remnants of ancient hedgerows.

Whinchat Ridge

On Mynydd y Garn Fawr, an ongoing and recurring problem has risen regarding the regeneration of lodgepole pines from a nearby plantation. The problem is continuously being redressed. Other species of bird that are the whinchat's neighbours during the breeding season includes the numerous and highly successful meadow pipit, skylark, linnet, tree pipit, reed bunting, stonechat, willow warbler, wren, blackbird and cuckoo. Occasional and rarer species are grasshopper warbler, Dartford warbler, and common whitethroat. Birds of prey may include hobby, buzzard, sparrowhawk, kestrel, merlin, peregrine, short-eared owl and hen harrier.

Other wildlife to inhabit the moor includes fox, stoat, weasel, adder and common lizard. The district is grazed by sheep at a low to medium level, and locally by cattle and semi wild ponies in very small numbers.

Some management of the moorland tops is ongoing, in the form of heather burning to promote regrowth of that vegetation type for red grouse.

Welsh Report 4

Methods

Each year, around mid-April, an intensive search and monitoring programme begins. These early days of a moorland breeding season become a period of reintroduction between observer, the location and its inhabitants. During this time, attentions are focused on the already present stonechat, which is also being studied keenly. It is a good time to assess the local stonechat population and find most of the first clutches before the migrant whinchat arrives on the scene at the end of April. From the middle of May, however, the whinchat takes preference as its breeding activities escalate. Singing males are noted, along with any visual signs of active females, while each pair's territory is logged for future reference. From then on, the study area is walked on a regular basis and previously known and traditional nesting sites are methodically searched and revisited during a time of much activity. The nests are discovered using tried and tested methods and field craft skills and the contents are recorded along with any other data such as the nest site vegetation. The young are preferably ringed around one week old and it is at this time that an attempt to trap the adult pair near the nest is made. This is achieved using baited 'potter' traps, which are set on the ground near the nest or close to one or more of the pair's favourite perches. All nests are thereafter revisited at least once to assess success. At those sites where a breeding attempt has failed, there is usually another attempt by a determined pair. With this scenario comes the repeated possibility of trapping adult birds missed previously. The whinchat breeding season is never regarded as over until the last day of July and the study area is visited on many occasions to determine that all available data has been collected and nothing has been missed.

In the early days of the study, a colour coding scheme was operational. However, after six years without any feedback, other than my own, and a few problems with the plastic rings, this was discontinued. During the early stages of the study, a compass was regularly used to determine the direction in which the nest entrance was facing.

The Breeding Season

The male whinchat arrives back in the study area in the last week of April (mean 26th, 1990-2000). Traditional territorial sites are taken up and singing commences in order to defend chosen sites and to attract the females which arrive between a few days and a week or so later. Eggs can be expected from the middle of May onwards. Six is the most common first clutch size though 4-7 are frequent. The overall mean clutch size for 1991-2001, including all locations within the study area, is 5.3. The breeding season has two discernible peaks (fig 1), the young are born generally from the first week of June and from then on, this month is by far the busiest in the life cycle of the whinchat. The average mean brood size at the time of ringing is 5.1 and the young are in the nest for about thirteen days. However, a well-fed brood may leave when as young as eight days old if disturbed. There is a small resurgence in activity in early to mid-July when replacement or second clutches/broods are found. Very few of these late nests are actual true second breeding attempts but are replacements for earlier failures. The season is effectively over at the end of July when only one or two broods can still be found in the nest.

Welsh Report 5

Fig. 1. The timing of the Whinchat breeding season.

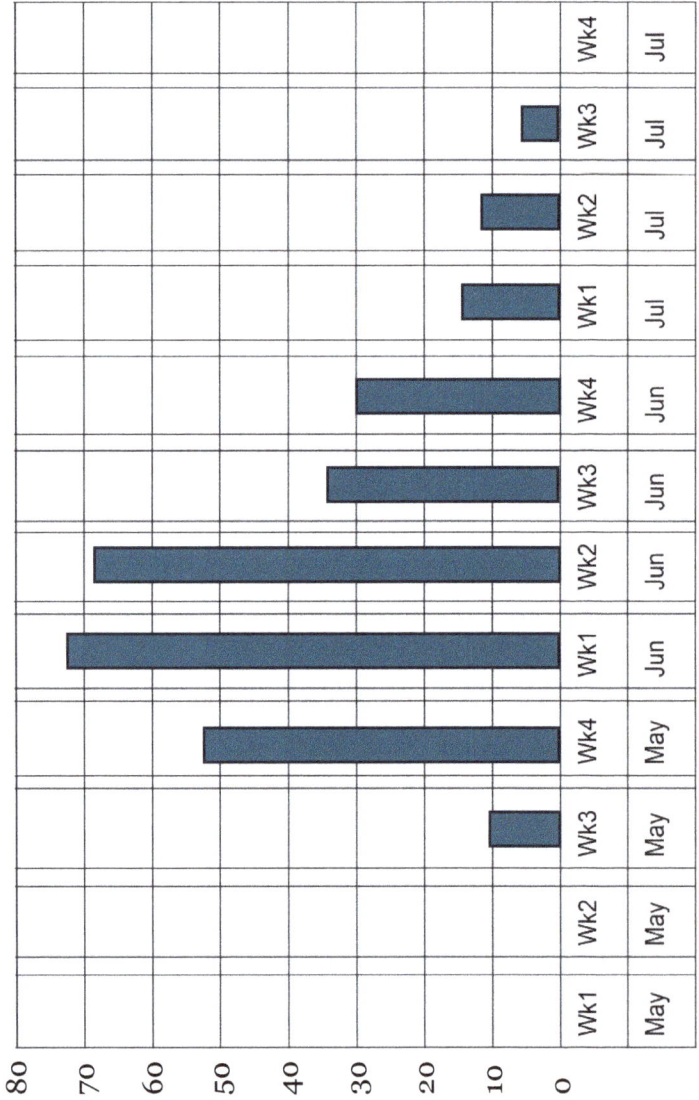

Whinchat Ridge

Breeding Densities

The overall density of breeding whinchat at various sites within the study area is governed by a variety of factors e.g. the vegetation type within a given area, elevation, exposure, dampness etc. For example, Mynydd Garn Clochdy consists of 285 hectares overall, although only 160 hectares could be considered suitable for breeding whinchats. Garn Clochdy's average of 29 breeding pairs shows a density 1pr/5.5 hectares overall and 1 pr/3.8 ha at more productive sites. The Mynydd y Garn Fawr section covers 37.5 hectares and holds an average of 14 pairs per season. The density on Garn Fawr is 1pr/2.6 ha. Like Garn Clochdy, the bulk of the whinchat population can be found around the 400-metre contour line. The Blorenge covers 125 hectares of suitable habitat and with an average population 37.6 pairs produces a density of 1pr/3.3 ha.

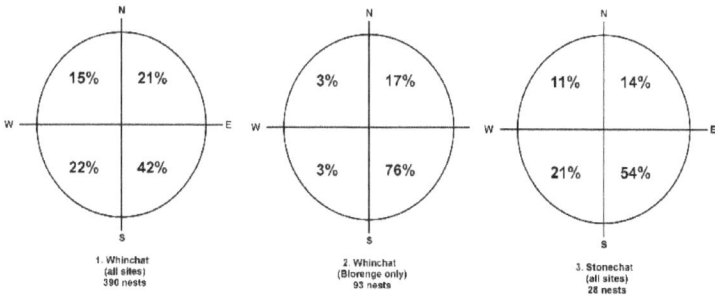

1. Whinchat (all sites) 390 nests

2. Whinchat (Blorenge only) 93 nests

3. Stonechat (all sites) 28 nests

Welsh Report 6

Nesting Sites

Data involving choice of nesting site are collected at every location. Data gathered from the start of the study in 1994, and based on information from 376 nest sites, indicated that bilberry was the favoured vegetation type in which the whinchat built its nest. A total of 246 nests (65%) were found in sites where bilberry was the dominant vegetation, while bracken 44 nests (12%), was the nearest 'rival'. Heather, though a common plant at all sites, was represented by only 23 nests (6%), roughly the same figures as for crowberry and grass species. Though these figures are of a historical nature, they remain typical to the present day with the whinchat showing a huge preference for bilberry as a nesting site in the study area. Of course, at most sites, there is a variety of vegetation types. At another whinchat study location on the Powys border[11], it relies heavily on bracken which is by far the most available vegetation type present there. Some of this bracken is very sparse, even at nesting time, resulting in very little cover for the nest, unlike the protection provided by bilberry at the Gwent location. Indeed, it is here in Gwent that areas of bracken have been the first to be abandoned by the whinchat as the numbers of breeding pairs have diminished in some districts. From the start of the study, the direction the nest was facing was recorded. Data collected was inconclusive and irregular at first, but an interesting pattern has since emerged, showing a strong south-easterly preference. (See fig. 2.)

---

[11] M. Lawrence

Welsh Report 7

Ringing

A total of c 900 whinchat nests has been monitored, more than 3,000 young have been ringed since a ringing programme was initiated in 1989. Over 400 adult birds have been processed to the present day (2003) while 800 birds were colour-ringed in the early 1990s.

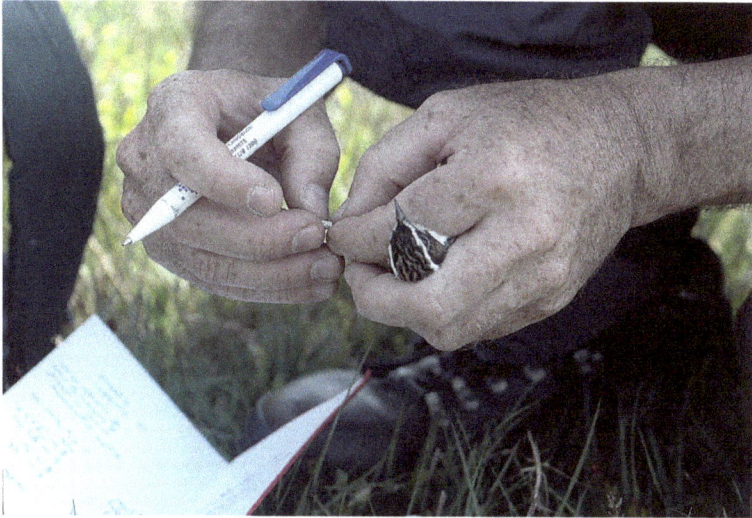

The main objective of the intensive ringing schedule at present is to contribute to the RAS project organised by the BTO to determine the survival rate of the breeding whinchats within the study area. Between 1993 and 2001, 430 adult birds were trapped. The sexes of the birds caught were evenly represented, (210 male, 220 female). The re-trap rate has risen annually since the RAS project started in 1998. (1998=25%, 1999=34%, 2000=47%, 2001=70%). Again, the sexes were evenly represented with 87 re-traps for each sex since 1993, resulting in a 50% re-trap rate for both male and female, indicating an even balance toward site loyalty. A similar whinchat study in Powys[12] produced four controls for the Gwent RAS study in 2001 when three of the Powys-ringed birds showed up 16km away at the Gwent site after a migration. All three birds were breeding females. It was the first known controls from the Powys study to breed at the Gwent location since the respective studies began. Other noteworthy occurrences involved a control of a breeding male on the Blorenge mountain, which was originally ringed in Cambridge. The only foreign recovery to date is of a young bird ringed on Mynydd y Garn Fawr in June 1999 and subsequently recorded in the south of France near the Pyrenees only 58 days later. There is also a longevity record of a male recorded four times in six years on the Blorenge.

Ringing has also produced recoveries from an unlikely source. During 2000-01, a study which involved searching old and new sparrowhawk nesting sites was undertaken[13]; to date, 15 rings involving six species have been located, some in the nest of the raptor, some in pellets, and some buried in the leaf litter. Eleven of the rings found were originally fitted to whinchats within the study area.

[12] M. Lawrence
[13] Smith & Lawrence

Welsh Report 8

Discussion

As with so many migrant and resident species alike, the whinchat is, in the opinion of the author, becoming scarcer, particularly at a local level. Though still a relatively common breeding species in its favoured habitat, the vulnerability of the whinchat is highlighted by its past track-record of becoming absent as a breeding bird from various lowland and farmland habitats in fairly recent times. In the study area, the population seems to be receding from its southernmost outposts. The reasons for this are yet unknown, although there may be a few contributing factors locally. Numbers also fluctuate annually due to a succession of unseasonable weather patterns. Figure 3 opposite gives breeding success data in summarised form for the years 1998-2001 as examples.

Fig. 3.

MYNYDD GARN CLOCHDY 1998-2001

Date Year	Pairs	Nests	Eggs	Average Clutch	Young Hatched	% Hatched	Fledged	% Fledged	% Success
1998	29	36	192	5.3	163	85	134	82	70
1999	32	30	156	5.2	143	92	129	90	83
2000	30	31	159	5.1	129	81	78	60	49
2001	25	22	121	5.5	101	83	84	83	69
Total	29 av	30 av	157 av	5.2	134 av	85	106 av	79	68

BLORENGE MOUNTAIN 1998-2001

Date Year	Pairs	Nests	Eggs	Average Clutch	Young Hatched	% Hatched	Fledged	% Fledged	% Success
1998	35	28	163	5.8	151	93	135	89	83
1999	40	36	196	5.4	185	94	165	89	84
2000	40	30	151	5.0	148	98	122	82	81
2001	33	26	149	5.7	140	94	124	89	83
Total	37 av	30 av	165 av	5.4	156 av	95	137 av	88	83

Welsh Report 9.

MYNYDD Y GARN FAWR 1998-2001

Date Year	Pairs	Nests	Eggs	Average Clutch	Young Hatched	% Hatched	Fledged	% Fledged	% Success
1998	21	21	111	5.2	104	94	83	80	75
1999	14	13	62	4.7	52	84	44	85	71
2000	15	17	83	4.8	71	86	56	79	67
2001	13	12	68	5.6	61	90	41	67	60
Total	16 av	16 av	81 av	5.1	72 av	89	56 av	78	69

ALL SITES SUMMARY 1998-2001

Date Year	Pairs	Nests	Eggs	Average Clutch	Young Hatched	% Hatched	Fledged	% Fledged	% Success
1998	85	85	466	5.4	418	90	352	84	75
1999	86	79	414	5.2	380	92	337	89	81
2000	85	78	393	5.0	348	89	256	74	65
2001	71	60	338	5.6	302	80	249	82	74
Total	327	302	1611		1448		1194		
Av	82	75	403	5.3	362	90	298	82	74

Steve J Smith

Welsh Report 10

Recent colder/wetter summers in the hills have resulted in poor reproduction success rates, due to such climate changes. Also, a higher than normal predation rate in some districts may have reduced the numbers of young birds able to return as breeding adults loyal to their place of birth. There has been little habitat change within the study area. Although there has been some forestry encroachment, there is still plenty of room for a healthy population to survive. Grazing by sheep and cattle is minimal, though a possible problem is with habitat destruction where farmers continually use certain, relatively small areas of prime habitat as winter gathering and feeding areas for livestock. This is something there must be a compromise on because the survival of the livestock depends on it. Human disturbance is on the increase, especially on the Blorenge Mountain, where vehicular access is available. The whinchat also has many possible enemies in the form of avian and mammalian predators, many of which seem to be thriving during this period of milder winters. It has been proved in a recent study[14], that the sparrowhawk is having a significant effect on the study species and others, especially in those areas of moorland that are overlooked by forestry plantations where the Sparrowhawk prefers to nest.

Competition for nesting sites is not an issue as the whinchat appears to be higher in the 'pecking order' than most of its neighbours, with only the stonechat showing any signs of supremacy in the form of aggressive dominance over the whinchat. The numbers of breeding stonechat are comparatively low, however, and are therefore a limited problem. The effects on the migratory population and the stability of the species in its African wintering grounds are unknown to date.

---

[14] Smith & Lawrence 2002

138

The Atlas of Gwent Birds

Below are some of the notes that were written by me to describe the whinchat's status in Gwent and South Wales. The information was gathered in support of the production of the Atlas of Gwent Birds.

The Birds of Wales 1992-2000[15] has described the population of breeding whinchats as declining and predominately a species of upland areas. There are signs that the whinchat is declining slightly from its strongholds, although numbers fluctuate annually. Welsh common bird survey results indicated a national decline of 16-20% since 1991 and the population was therefore estimated at 2,400 pairs only. However, I suggest a more realistic figure of around 5,000 pairs[16]. This mirrors the whinchat status in Gwent where, historically, it is a species that has seen decline in breeding numbers from the coastal levels and the lowland habitats in general. The whinchat now resides in the hills to the north and west of the county.

The moorland edges and the hill-sides where there are deep gullies and the land undulates to give shelter and adequate nesting sites in the favourite haunt of the whinchat, especially where the vegetation type includes bilberry, bracken and heather. Bracken is often associated with the whinchat and *vice versa*. The whinchat also benefitted initially from the planting of coniferous forests in the uplands but the local populations were prone to crash as the trees grew larger and relinquished any benefits they once held for the chats as suitable breeding habitat.

Humphrey's *Birds of Monmouthshire 1963* describes the whinchat as breeding regularly on the coastal flats, railway embankments and other lowland habitats as well as in the

---

[15] Green et al for Welsh Ornithological Society
[16] As quoted by Lovegrove et al in the *Birds of Wales 1994.*

hills. Up until the early 1970s there were still some sporadic breeding records in lowland districts; however, such records are rare these days.

The whinchat has been a largely under-studied species in Gwent until recent times. Regular counts were apparent from St. Mary's Vale during the 1970s onward, while 20 pairs were noted in the Twmbarlwm hills at Cwm Lickey (O'Duffy, *Gwent Bird Report 1985*). Boyland (*GBR 1980*) estimated a breeding population of 77 pairs along the 220-metre contour of the Henllys to Penyrheol ridge. Ten broods were ringed at Trefil in 1998 by M. Lawrence as part of his study which was mainly conducted in Powys. Smith (1986-present) has studied all aspects of the whinchat breeding biology and this has been supported by an intensive ringing programme and has produced breeding figures for the Blorenge (37.6 av. Prs, 1pr. Per 3.3 hec.), Mynydd y Garn Fawr (14.0 av. Prs, 1 pr per 2.6 hec.), Mynydd Garn Clochdy (29 av. Prs, 1 pr per 5.5 hec.) and Coity mountain ridges (25 prs.). However, the breeding population in many parts of Gwent has largely gone unchecked.

Records for the 1982-85 period for the first *Gwent Atlas* recorded in the breeding season in 88 tetrads[17] while 42 of these tetrads contained confirmed breeding pairs. While whinchats occupied 76 tetrads during the data collecting period for the new *Atlas*, confirmed breeding was represented in 45 tetrads. Subsequently, these figures would confirm the trend of a decreasing population. Though numbers can fluctuate, any local recovery of breeding populations has gone unaided in recent years following a series of cooler, wetter summers.

On average, the whinchat arrives back in its breeding grounds in the third week of April with a steady flow of birds into the first week of May. Any March sightings are debatable and very unlikely. There is a definite movement away from the hillside breeding grounds from as early as the end of June

---

[17] An area 2 km x 2 km square

and early July (despite some birds still nesting) when individuals and family groups of whinchat are recorded at localities such as Llandegfedd Reservoir and various inland farmland sites throughout the county. The movement of passage off the mountains can, however, continue through August and September and even linger into early October, although by then migration has long been under way. This is strongly apparent by the presence of whinchats along the Gwent coast throughout September and October, with occasional November records (debatable, in my view)[18]. There have been several historical records of birds on the coast during the winter months, such as 3rd January 1966, 6th December 1970, November-end of year 1982, and December 1992.

---

[18] The only explanations for the winter records, in my opinion, is mis-identification or the observation of birds not fit enough to migrate.

Acknowledgements

My acknowledgments and heartfelt thanks go out to the following:

Rhiannon Chandler, for being the first person to read the original draft and for her advice and encouragement.

Mark Lawrence, memory maker and one of the best birders I've ever met.

Steve Williams, lifelong friend and caring naturalist. There from the start.

Kevin Smith, my brother, for the memories of the camping trips and early nest finding forays

Jim Rawlings for birding forays late into the evening, watching whinchats as the sun went down.

Kevin Richards, a man with true hunting instincts and perfect working companion.

Dave Lock, bird photographer with a caring nature. Whose knowledge and compassion for his subject is second to none.

Percy Playford, my dear late school master, friend and mentor. Thank you for the lifelong memories and inspiration.

Dr Stephanie Tyler MBE, one of the hardest working naturalists I've ever met not enough can be said about how you inspire me.

Alyson, Sarah and Stephanie, my wife and daughters whose love and support carries me through whatever I do in my life.

Mam and Dad, the anchors of a very happy and fruitful life. Dad, for the birds in my blood and Mam for always being there and for loving me wholeheartedly.

Steve J Smith

Heather, my collie dog who shared my journey without question for the love of life and to please me unconditionally. Forever in my thoughts.

Penny and Julie at Saron Publishers, who have become friends. I thank them for their unwavering support and belief in my little book. Without their professional nurturing of my writing and understanding of my yearning to put my life's work to paper, this book would simply still be gathering dust.

The Whinchat species, my obsession, my inspiration, my lifelong passion. We've shared the good times and the bad. I've wept for you and felt your hardship and my respect for you will continue to grow for the remainder of my days.

References

Smith S.J. & Lawrence M.: *Ringing Recoveries at Sparrowhawk Sites - The Impact on Whinchats.* BTO. (2002)

Tyler S.J., Lewis J., Venables A. and Walton J.: *The Gwent Atlas of Breeding Birds.* GOS. (1987)

Tyler S.J. et al.: *Population Estimates of Birds in Gwent. Welsh Birds Vol 1 No.2 1995*

Various: *Whinchat summary. (Boyland) GOS. Gwent Bird Report, 1981 edition*

Various: *Gwent Bird Report, 1994 edition. GOS.*

www.ingramcontent.com/pod-product-compliance
Lightning Source LLC
Chambersburg PA
CBHW051246020426
42333CB00025B/3077